THE

PRESBYTERIAN MANUAL:

CONTAINING

FORMS FOR THE RECORDS

OF THE

SESSION, PRESBYTERY, AND SYNOD;

AND FOR

THE JUDICIAL AND OTHER ECCLESIASTICAL PROCEEDINGS
REQUIRED BY THE POLITY

OF THE

Presbyterian Church.

BY

REV. JOHN N. LEWIS,

LATELY STATED CLERK OF THE SYNOD OF NEW YORK AND NEW JERSEY.

PHILADELPHIA:
PRESBYTERIAN PUBLICATION COMMITTEE,
1334 CHESTNUT STREET.
NEW YORK: A. D. F. RANDOLPH, 683 BROADWAY.
CINCINNATI: WM. SCOTT....ST. LOUIS: J. W. McINTYRE....DETROIT:
RAYMOND & LAPHAM....CHICAGO: WM. TOMLINSON.

STEREOTYPED BY L. JOHNSON & CO.
PHILADELPHIA.

CONTENTS.

PREFACE.

THE Manual which is herewith presented to the Church is believed to be the only book of its class.

The labor of preparing it was undertaken by the Rev. John N. Lewis, at the request of a Committee of the General Assembly.

The original design was to append the "forms" to the new Digest of the Acts and Decisions of the Assembly, which the committee had been appointed to arrange. When, however, it was ascertained that the Digest must be made so much more voluminous than was at first intended, Mr. Lewis was requested to enlarge the plan of the Manual, and to prepare it for publication as a separate and independent work.

The labor expended upon this volume has been by no means inconsiderable; but it is believed that the attention thus bestowed by one so eminently qualified by experience and information for the task, has been well spent. The Manual will meet the wants of a multitude of Presbyterian ministers and elders, and prove to them a great saving of time and trouble. To know *how to do a thing rightly at first* is a privilege which will be appreciated by those whose lot it has been to halt for lack of this information with regard to the details of ministerial and official duties. In other departments books of forms have long been used, and are considered indispensable; but for ecclesiastical proceedings no "Clerk's Assistant" has been put forth. "THE PRESBYTERIAN MANUAL" will doubtless prove acceptable and helpful to office-bearers in all branches of the Presbyterian Church.

J. W. D.

THE PRESBYTERIAN MANUAL.

Form for the Records of a Session.

E——, January 1, 18—.

PURSUANT to the call of the Moderator, the Session met in the church, after the Preparatory Lecture, and was opened with prayer.

Present,—the Rev. A. B., Moderator,
Mr. C. D.,
" E. F.,
" G. H.,
" I. K.—Elders.

Absent,—Dr. L. J. and Mr. M. N.

The minutes of the last meeting were read and approved.

Mr. H. gave his reason for being absent from the last meeting of the Session; which was sustained.

L. M., and C. his wife, and N. O., appeared before the Session as candidates for admission to the full communion of the Church, and O. R., and S., the wife of T. E., (both unbaptized,) as candidates for admission to the privileges of church-membership.*

They were severally examined respecting their experimental acquaintance with the Christian religion, their approval of the doctrinal standards of the Presbyterian Church, and their readiness to submit themselves to the discipline of Christ's house; and, their examination having been sustained, it was

---

* The different forms of expression in this minute are intended to mark the important—albeit too much neglected—distinction between the children of the Church and the people of the world,—though the latter may be regular attendants upon public worship, and connected with the religious society as known to the civil law.

The *former*, having been born within the pale of the visible kingdom of Christ, are to be recognised as the *infant members* of his Church. As such, they have a *right* to receive "the seal of the covenant," and to enjoy all the privileges appropriate to this infant relation, including the special oversight, instructions, and prayers, as well as the affectionate interest of the pastor, the elders, and the whole body of Christ; and when they arrive at *Christian* maturity, indicated not so much by the amount as by the satisfactory evidence of the *reality* of their Christian experience, they are to be received into the *full communion* of the Church.

The *latter*, having no birthright privileges in the Church of Christ, may be considered as "proselytes of the gate;" who, on exhibiting credible evidence of "repentance toward God and faith toward our Lord Jesus Christ," may be admitted, as "proselytes of righteousness," to the *privileges of church-membership*, including the sacraments and the brotherhood of the people of God.

Resolved, That the candidates be received on the next Sabbath, upon their publicly assenting to the Confession and Covenant of this Church.

J. B. presented his certificate of dismission and recommendation from the Presbyterian church in H——, N.Y., and requested that he might be admitted to the membership of this church.

The certificate was found to be in order, and the request of Mr. B. was granted.

D. Y. presented a similar request, accompanied by a certificate from the Congregational church in C——, Conn.

His certificate having been found to be in order, his request was granted.

R. C. requested a certificate of dismission from this church, and of recommendation to the Presbyterian church in N——, Pa. His request was granted.

Mr. D. reported that he had attended the stated autumnal meeting of the Presbytery at M., and also the adjourned meeting at D., and the special meeting at G.

Mr. H. reported that he had attended the annual sessions of the Synod at P——, N.Y.

Mr. F. was appointed to represent this Session at the stated spring meeting of the Presbytery, and Dr. J. was appointed his alternate.

The following minute was adopted, namely:—

In view of the inadequate supply of psalm-books in our congregation, and of the fact that "The Church Psalmist" has been adopted by our General Assembly as their Book of Psalms and Hymns for use in church worship, and that it is issued by our Publication Committee,

Resolved, That we adopt "The Church Psalmist," and that Mr. F. be a committee to ascertain upon what terms a supply of the book, in different sizes, can be procured.

Messrs. D. and N. were appointed a committee to examine the condition of the Sabbath-school connected with this congregation; and to report, at the next meeting of the Session, what measures, if any, can be adopted to promote the efficiency of that important institution.

The Moderator and Messrs. K. and F. were appointed a committee to rearrange our scheme of collections in aid of the several religious benevolent societies, with a view to secure the more general and more liberal co-operation of the members of the congregation.

The Session then adjourned.

Concluded with prayer.

A. B., *Moderator*, [or E. F., *Clerk.*]

Informal Meetings of the Session.

[The exigencies of business, as well as the circumstances of the several elders, often make it convenient for the pastor to call a meeting of the Session at the close of some religious service, when time is not afforded for holding a *formal* meeting and the nature of the business to be transacted does not render it essential. In such cases, the matter may be acted upon without delay, and the record may be appropriately entered upon the minutes of the next regular meeting, in the following form:—]

It appeared that, at certain informal meetings of the Session, holden since the last regular meeting, D. K., and P. his wife, were dismissed, and recommended to the Presbyterian church in W——, N.J.:—Mr. D. was appointed to represent this Session in the stated autumnal meeting of the Presbytery, and Mr. F. was appointed his alternate:—and Mr. H. was appointed the delegate to attend the annual meeting of the Synod, and Dr. J. was appointed his alternate.

Whereupon, it was

Resolved, That the above proceedings of the informal meetings be approved and entered upon the minutes.

[The appropriate place for this minute is immediately after the record of the excuses of absentees; or, if there is no such record, it should follow that of the reading and approval of the minutes.

The order of time should always be preserved in such a minute; and the several items of business should be carefully separated from each other, as above, by a colon and dash.

If a single informal meeting only has been holden, the minute should be commenced,—]

It appeared that, at an informal meeting holden, &c.

[If only one item of business has been attended to in this manner, the *resolution* should be expressed,—]

Resolved, That the above action of the informal meeting be approved and entered upon the minutes.

Minutes respecting the Election of Additional Elders.

[A matter of so great concern as the election of additional elders will naturally be made the subject of conversation in the Session, and probably at several meetings, before it will be advisable to take notice of it in the minutes. When, however, the opinions of the several members begin to assume a more definite form and to approach a harmonious result, it will be proper to introduce the subject in a formal manner, which may be done by the following minute:—]

The subject of an increase of the eldership in this church, having been discussed informally at several recent meetings of the Session, was again taken up for consideration, and

The remainder of the meeting was spent in consultation upon this important subject:

Pending which,

The Session adjourned, to meet on [Monday] next, at, &c.

[At the adjourned meeting, after recording the preliminary business, the minutes may proceed, as follows:—]

The unfinished business of the last meeting—namely, the subject of an increase of the eldership in this church—was then taken up for consideration.

After a full and free interchange of opinion, it was

Resolved, As the unanimous judgment of the Session, that the welfare of this church, and the interests of religion within our bounds, render it expedient that the number of the eldership should be increased, without unnecessary delay.

Resolved, That the Session will, and hereby does, recommend to the church the election of —— additional ruling elders.

Resolved, further, as the deliberate, cordial, and unanimous judgment of the Session, That the following named persons—all being "male members in full communion in this church"—be, and the same hereby are, nominated to the church as candidates for election to the office of ruling elder, namely:—

Messrs. R. B., T. L. C., and P. S.

Messrs. K. and D. were appointed a committee to wait upon the candidates above named, and to inform them of the purpose of the Session to nominate them to the church for the purpose aforesaid, and also to obtain, if possible, their acceptance of the nomination.

[At a subsequent meeting, the committee being prepared to report, the following record should be made :—]

The committee appointed to wait upon the candidates for nomination to the eldership reported, that it has performed the duty which was assigned to it by the Session, and that the candidates have all signified their acceptance of the nomination.

The report was accepted; and,

In view thereof, it was

Resolved, That the nomination of the said candidates be presented to the church on the next Sabbath, and that it be repeated on the Sabbath following.

Resolved, That the election for ruling elders be holden in the lecture-room, at the close of the first weekly lecture after the nomination shall have been published the second time; and that notice to that effect be given from the pulpit at each time of publishing the nomination.

Resolved, That the candidates, if they shall

be elected by the church, be ordained to the office of ruling elder on the —— Sabbath in —— next. [or inst.]

[The candidates having been elected and ordained, a meeting of the Session should be holden, on the earliest convenient day, for the purpose of receiving and enrolling the new elders.

After the reading of the minutes, and the excuses of absentees, the record should proceed as follows:—]

It appeared that the brethren nominated by the Session as candidates for the office of ruling elder, having been duly and unanimously elected by the church,

Were solemnly ordained to that office on the Sabbath, the —— day of —— inst.

The new elders, being present to-day, were cordially welcomed to their seats as members of this Session; and

Their names are now enrolled, as follows, namely:—

Mr. R. B.,
" T. L. C.,
" P. S.—Elders.

Minute respecting the Death of a Ruling Elder.

[The following minute is recommended as being sufficiently full, unless in very extraordinary cases, and as avoiding the liability to invidious distinctions, against which great care should always be taken to guard the records of deliberative, and especially of ecclesiastical bodies.]

Our esteemed brother, Mr. P. D., having been removed by death since the last regular meeting of the Session,

The following minute is unanimously adopted, namely:—

With humble submission to the dispensation of God's holy providence, the Session records the death of one of its members,—Mr. P. D., —who departed this life on [Friday] the —— day of —— inst., [or ult.,] in the —— year of his age.

Minute respecting the Death of a Pastor.

[The sentiment of the note prefixed to the minute respecting the death of a ruling elder has influenced the preparation of that now given. In all such cases, a true taste will indicate simplicity rather than panegyric.]

The Rev. C. D., the pastor of this congregation, having been removed by death since the last regular meeting of the Session,

The following minute is unanimously adopted, namely:—

With humble submission to the dispensation of God's holy providence, the Session records the death of the Rev. C. D., the beloved and lamented pastor of this congregation, who departed this life on [Monday] the —— day of —— inst., [or ult.,] in the —— year of his age and the —— of his ministry; having been the faithful pastor of this congregation for the space of — years.

Minutes respecting the Temporary Supply of a Vacant Pulpit.

[When the vacancy has been occasioned by the *death* of the pastor, the following minute should succeed the one in which the formal record of the death is made:—]

The following minute also was adopted:—

The pulpit of this church having been now made vacant by the decease of our pastor, it has become the duty of the Session to provide for the regular maintenance of the ordinances of public worship, until God, in his great mercy, shall send to us another pastor, in whom the hearts of our bereaved congregation may be united.

Be it, therefore,

Resolved, That Messrs. D. and H. be appointed a committee to procure supplies for the pulpit, that the people may not be deprived of the means of grace in their accustomed place of public worship.

Resolved, That the Committee of Supplies be directed to present a respectful request to the

Presbytery for the appointment of occasional supplies, from its own members, for our pulpit; provided, that at the time of the next meeting of the Presbytery there shall appear to be no immediate prospect of our obtaining a pastor.

Resolved, if the Board of Trustees shall concur, That the treasurer of the congregation be authorized and directed to pay to the ministers who may occupy the pulpit during the time of its continuing vacant, the sum of ten dollars for each Sabbath's services, and of five dollars for each Preparatory Lecture, together with a suitable allowance for their travelling expenses.

[If the vacancy shall have been occasioned by the *resignation* of the pastor, the fact of the dissolution of the pastoral relation, and of the consequent vacancy, may most appropriately be brought upon the records of the Session in the report of the elder who represented the church in the Presbytery at the time of its action in the premises. The record should be :—]

Mr. D. reported that he had attended the special meeting of the Presbytery, holden at D., which was called for the purpose of dismissing our esteemed pastor,—the Rev. C. D., —who has felt it to be his duty to resign his pastoral relation to this congregation, &c.

[This minute may be completed, according to the facts, by adding—On account of protracted and serious indisposition; —or, in order that he may enter upon another sphere of service,

&c.;—or, in order that he may become the pastor of the church in ——. Then let the record proceed:—]

Whereupon the following minute was adopted, namely:—

The pulpit of this church having been made vacant by the dismission of our pastor, it has become the duty of the Session to provide for the regular maintenance of the ordinances of public worship, until God, in his great mercy, shall send to us another pastor, in whom the people of this congregation may become united.

[The same resolutions should then follow as in the preceding formula.]

[At the first meeting of the Session holden after the resignation or death of the pastor, it should, without fail, elect a *Stated Clerk,* unless it already has such an officer. The following is a suitable record to be made of his election; and it should immediately succeed the resolutions respecting the supply of the pulpit:—]

Mr. E. F. was then elected to the office of Stated Clerk of this Session.

After which,

The Session adjourned.

Concluded with prayer.

E. F., *Stated Clerk.*

Minutes respecting the Election of a Pastor.

[It is provided in the "Form of Government," chap. xv. sec. i., that when "the people appear prepared to elect a pastor, the Session shall take measures to convene them for the purpose." In pursuance of this direction, the following record should be made:—]

The following minute was adopted:—

The Session, having reason to believe that the people of this congregation are prepared with a good degree of unanimity to elect a pastor, adopted the following resolutions, namely:—

Resolved, That a meeting of the congregation, for the election of a pastor, be holden in the church on Wednesday, the —— inst.; and that the notice of this meeting be given from the pulpit on the next Sabbath, in accordance with the "Form of Government," chap. xv. sec. iii.

Resolved, That the Stated Clerk be directed to invite the Rev. R. A. to attend the meeting of the congregation, and to preside in the proposed election of a pastor.

[When a pastor shall have been elected by the congregation, and the candidate shall have intimated his willingness to accept the "call," if a regular or an adjourned meeting of the Presbytery is near at hand, no further action by the Session will be necessary, as "commissioners to prosecute the call" before the

Presbytery ought always to be appointed by the congregation. But if it shall appear to be desirable that a *special* meeting of the Presbytery should be holden to install the pastor, the Session should take order, as embodied in the following minute, which may be passed at an "informal meeting," and entered upon the records as directed in the formula under that head:—]

Messrs. F. and H. were appointed a committee to take the necessary measures for convening a special meeting of the Presbytery for the installation of our pastor elect; and also to make arrangements for the entertainment of the members of Presbytery when they shall be assembled here.

[At the first meeting of the Session holden after the installation of the pastor, the elder who represented the church in the Presbytery should make his report, which may be entered upon the record thus:—]

Mr. D. reported that he had attended the adjourned [or special] meeting of the Presbytery, which was holden in this place on Wednesday, the —— day of —— inst., [or ult.,] for the purpose of installing the Rev. A. B. as the pastor of this congregation.

A Certificate of Dismission.

E——, January 1, 186—.

This is to certify that R. C. is a member in good standing of the First Presbyterian

Church of A——, and that he is hereby dismissed at his own request, and affectionately recommended to the fellowship of the Presbyterian church in N——, Pa., or of any other church in our communion, with which God, in his providence, may order his lot, and when so received his responsibility to this church will cease.

By order of Session.

A. B., *Moderator.*

This certificate is valid only for one year from its date, "except where there is no opportunity of presenting it to a church." See Book of Discipline, chap. xi. sec. ii.

[When the person dismissed is a ruling elder, the following paragraph may be added to the above certificate :—]

It is proper to add that Mr. C. has, for the space of —— years, sustained the office of ruling elder, to the edification of the church, and enjoyed the fraternal confidence and affection of his brethren in the eldership.

[When the person dismissed is a deacon, the same paragraph may be added to the certificate, only substituting the title "*deacon*" for that of "*ruling elder,*" and for the words "*of his brethren in the Session*" the words "*of its officers.*"]

[When the person dismissed has "neglected, for a reasonable time, to apply for" a certificate, the Book of Discipline directs (chap. xi. secs. iii. and iv.) that the certificate shall not endorse "his demeanor" during the interval, "unless the judicatory have good information of a more recent date." In ordinary cases here contemplated, it will be sufficient to add to the first clause of the foregoing certificate, after the word "standing,"]

Up to the time of his removal from our bounds.

A Letter of Credence.

E——, January 1, 18—.

This is to certify that H. N. is a member of the [First] Presbyterian Church in this [village], in good and regular standing.

As he contemplates spending some [weeks] in journeying, this Letter of Credence is given to him, that it may introduce him to the people of God, and facilitate his occasional communion with any church of our Lord and Saviour Jesus Christ among whom he may for the time be sojourning.

By order of the Session.

A. B., *Moderator.*

[In such a letter, if the person to whom it is given is an officer in the church, the title of his office—as ruling elder, or deacon—should be substituted in the first line for the word *member*.

A Letter of Credence may, in many cases, be appropriately given by the pastor, without the action of the Session. Its general introduction is earnestly recommended, as adapted to promote the comfort of those who carry it, and to be, in many ways, of great utility.

Such a letter may also be given to a member of the church who is about to remove from its bounds, but who may not be able to designate, at the time, the church to which he will desire to be recommended. In such a case, the second paragraph should commence :—]

As he is about to remove [or, has removed] from our bounds, but has not yet been able to determine with what particular church to connect himself, this Letter of Credence, &c.

[In the case of a member *removing his residence* beyond the bounds of the church, as contemplated in the preceding formula, the following paragraph should be added to the letter, namely :—]

It is understood that, when he shall have located himself, he will, without delay, apply for a certificate of dismission from this church, that he may place himself regularly under the care of some evangelical church of Christ which may be convenient to his new residence.

Dedication of a House of Worship.

[After the sermon is ended, let the elders, the deacons, and the trustees arrange themselves in front of the pulpit, while the other heads of families rise in their places, or come forward, as may be convenient, that they may be addressed by the minister who is to offer the prayer of dedication. Then let the minister say :—]

According to the notice publicly given, we

have assembled to-day to dedicate this house to the worship of the only living and true God, —Jehovah, Father, Son, and Holy Ghost.

Now, if it is your desire that we should proceed to this service, let the officers of the church, and the trustees, together with all the members of the congregation, declare unto us, and say:—

Have you been moved to the erection of this edifice by a sincere desire to establish [or, to continue] among you the regular and solemn worship of the Most High God, for the spiritual benefit of yourselves and your families, and of this community?

Answer. We have.

Is it your sincere desire, and your solemn purpose, that this edifice shall be a house of worship, separated from secular uses, and devoted sacredly to the ordinances of religion, according to the customs and order of the Presbyterian Church in these United States?

Answer. It is.

Do you now, with one heart, give up this house to God, the Father, the Son, and the Holy Ghost, to be henceforth a house of prayer, a temple to his praise; and do you promise to provide for and to maintain here religious worship, seeing to it that nothing shall be wanting that may be needful for the decency, and propriety, and convenience thereof, according to the customs and order, as aforesaid, of the Presbyterian Church?

Answer. We do.

Blessed be the Lord God, who hath put it into your hearts to build this house unto his name. The Lord accept the labor of your hands, which you have offered unto him this day, and make good to you, and to your children after you, the word which he hath spoken:—"In all places where I record my name I will come unto thee, and I will bless thee!"

Let us pray.

[This order of dedication may be introduced at any part of the exercises, as may be deemed expedient; although the *most natural* place for the dedication is that already indicated,—"after the sermon."]

Form for the Minutes of a Presbytery.

STATED MEETING.

The Presbytery of H. met in the Presbyterian church in C. on Tuesday, April 17, 18—, at three o'clock, P.M., and was opened with a sermon by the Moderator, the Rev. A. B., from

1 Cor. iii. 11:—"For other foundation can no man lay than that is laid, which is Jesus Christ."

After the sermon, the Moderator offered prayer, and the Presbytery proceeded to the transaction of business.

The roll was made out, and is as follows:—*

MINISTERS.	CHURCHES.	ELDERS.
J. D.		
R. A.	C.	J. M.
A. B.	E.	E. F.
C. E.		
B. J.	B.	N. L.
	R.	B. D.
	W	L. K.

The following ministers were absent, namely:—the Rev. Messrs. O. R., D. P., and R. F.

The following churches were unrepresented, namely:—D., A., J., and M.

The Rev. B. J. was elected Moderator, and

* In making out the roll, the names of the ministers should always follow each other according to their seniority of ordination. The name of each church should be placed on the same line with that of its pastor or stated supply. The name of a minister without charge, or of one whose church is not represented, should not have that of a church on the same line; and a vacant church, or one whose pastor is absent, should occupy a line by itself,—as in the text.

the Rev. Messrs. R. A. and C. E. were elected Clerks.

The minutes of the last stated meeting, and also of the adjourned and special meetings, were read.

The members who had been absent from either of these meetings, and also the Sessions which had been unrepresented, were called upon for their excuses:—and

The excuses, having been rendered, were sustained.

The Rev. Messrs. D. O., of the Presbytery of L., R. K., of the Association of B., Mass., and W. R. N., of the Presbytery of T., being present, were invited to sit as corresponding members.

The docket of business was then presented, and read by the Stated Clerk.

The Treasurer presented his annual report, which, having been read, was referred to Messrs. L. and F., elders, for examination.

The Moderator gave notice that the Presbytery was ready to receive such letters and papers, designed to be brought before it for consideration, as may be in the hands of persons present.*

* The "Committee of Bills and Overtures" is deemed by some not unskilful in ecclesiastical matters to be unnecessary in a body whose members are so few as in many of our smaller

The Rev. D. O. presented a certificate of dismission and recommendation from the Presbytery of L., and requested that he may be received as a member of this Presbytery.

The certificate, having been read, was found to be in order, and the Rev. Mr. O. was received, according to his request.

A paper was presented purporting to be a call from the congregation in W. for the pastoral services of the Rev. D. O.; and

Messrs. L. K., N. M., and H. S. appeared before the Presbytery as commissioners on the

---

Presbyteries; and in its place this "call for papers" has been adopted.

According to this mode, business is introduced on the "call for papers," and may be either considered at once and decided, or placed upon the docket for future consideration, or referred to a special committee, on whose report the Presbytery proceeds to issue the matter.

When any of the "papers" presented are found to pertain to judicial business, a "judicial committee" should always be appointed, to which such papers should be referred at once, without reading, so that the "merits of a case" may not come prematurely before the body which may have to act judicially upon it.

The "call for papers" has been exhibited in the text, as a mode that has proved satisfactory where it has been adopted. Presbyteries which prefer making the appointment of the Committee of Bills and Overtures and the Judicial Committee as *standing committees*, are referred to the "Form for the Record of a Synod," in which the appointment and operation of these committees are fully given.

part of the congregation, appointed to prosecute the call.

The paper, having been read, was found to be in order; and, by the direction of the Presbytery, it was presented to the Rev. Mr. O. for his consideration.

The pastor elect then signified his acceptance of the call; and,

At the request of the commissioners, it was

Resolved, That the Presbytery will proceed to install the Rev. D. O., as pastor of the congregation in W., on the 2d day of May next, agreeably to the desire of the congregation; and

The Rev. Messrs. B. and O., and Mr. K., elder, were appointed a committee to make the necessary arrangements for the installation.

The Rev. R. K. presented a certificate of dismission and recommendation from the Association of B., Mass., and applied to be received as a member of this Presbytery.

The certificate was read, and was found to be in order.*

---

* Upon the application of a minister of another denomination for admission to a Presbytery, it is the privilege of members of the Presbytery to satisfy themselves, by inquiry of the applicant, as to his agreement with the doctrines held by the body.

The Moderator then proposed to the applicant the 2d, 3d, 4th, and 6th questions prescribed in the "Form of Government," chap. xv. sec. xii.

Satisfactory answers to these questions having been received,

The application of the Rev. R. K. was granted, and he was received [or enrolled] as a member of this Presbytery.

A recess was then taken until seven o'clock.

At seven o'clock the Rev. J. D. preached, according to appointment, on the doctrine of the Trinity, from 2 Cor. xiii. 14:—"The grace of the Lord Jesus Christ, and the love of God, and the communion of the Holy Ghost, be with you all. Amen."

After the services were concluded,

The Presbytery resumed the transaction of business.

The Rev. R. F. and Mr. J. R., elder from the church in M., appeared in the Presbytery, and gave their reasons for late attendance, which were sustained.

The Moderator announced the following committees*

* At this point, at the stated spring meeting, the Moderator should appoint a "Committee on the Minutes of the Synod,"

On the Records of the Sessions:

Of the Church in C.—The Rev. Mr. D., and Mr. L., elder.

Of the Church in E.—The Rev. Mr. A., and Mr. D., elder.

Of the Church in B.—The Rev. Mr. N., and Mr. K., elder.

Of the Church in R.—The Rev. Mr. K., and Mr. M., elder.

Of the Church in W.—The Rev. Mr. E., and Mr. R., elder.

Of the Church in M.—The Rev. Mr. O., and Mr. F., elder.

It was made the order of the day for to-morrow morning, at ten o'clock, to hear the Narratives of the State of Religion, and the Statistical Reports, of the several churches:—and

The Rev. Messrs. F. and B., and Mr. D., elder, were appointed the committee to prepare the Narrative of the State of Religion within the bounds of the Presbytery.

It was made the second order of the day for to-morrow morning, to elect commissioners to

---

if they have been printed; and, at the stated autumnal meeting, a "Committee on the Minutes of the General Assembly." For the appropriate minutes respecting such committees, and the action of the body on their reports, see the "Form for the Records of a Synod," pages —— and ——.

represent this Presbytery in the next General Assembly.

The Committee on Presbyterial Missions reported. Their report was accepted; and it was, unanimously,

Resolved, That the Presbytery renew its appointment of the Rev. B. B. as its missionary, to labor, as heretofore, within the bounds of this Presbytery, and at the same salary as the past year; and that the Committee on Presbyterial Missions consist of the same members as before, with the substitution of Rev. Mr. O. for Rev. J. T.

A communication was received from the General Assembly's Committee of Publication, respecting the objects and plans of the committee; and it was placed upon the docket for future consideration.

A paper was presented, which purported to be a complaint of certain parties in regard to the action of the Session of one of the churches under the care of this Presbytery.

The paper was referred to the Judicial Committee, to be appointed by the Moderator before the adjournment of the Presbytery this evening.

A request was received from the Session of the church in R., that the Presbytery will grant to them supplies for their pulpit for at least one Sabbath in each month, until the next stated meeting of the Presbytery.

The request was granted; and

The Rev. Messrs. E. and F., and Mr. D., the elder representing that Session, were appointed a committee to arrange the order in which the members shall supply the pulpit of the church in R.

The Moderator announced the Judicial Committee as follows, namely:—

The Rev. Messrs. B. and D., and Mr. R., elder.

The Presbytery then adjourned, to meet to-morrow morning, at eight o'clock, in this place.

Concluded with prayer.

Wednesday, April 18, 18—.

The Presbytery met, pursuant to its adjournment, and was opened with prayer.

The roll was then called; and, in addition to the members present yesterday, the Rev. D. P., and Messrs. B. W., elder from the church in A., and E. N., elder from the church in J., appeared in the Presbytery, and gave the reasons for their previous absence; which were sustained.

The minutes of the proceedings of yesterday were read and approved.

The examination of candidates for licensure

to preach the gospel was made the order of the day for two o'clock this afternoon.

Mr. K., elder, and the Rev. Mr. P., were appointed a committee to nominate a preacher, and to propose a subject for the discourse to be delivered on the Tuesday evening of the stated autumnal meeting of the Presbytery.

The committee to audit the Treasurer's accounts presented the following report, namely:—

The committee to which the Treasurer's accounts were referred for examination begs leave respectfully to report, that, having carefully examined the said accounts, it finds them to be correct, as compared with the vouchers accompanying them. To this report the committee, having been advised by the Treasurer that the balance in his hands is not sufficient to meet the incidental expenses of the Presbytery, would add the recommendation, that a tax of one dollar should be collected from each of the churches.

The report was accepted, and the recommendation of the committee was adopted.

Mr. W., elder, was appointed a committee to collect the amount specified from the elders present.

Mr. N., elder, stated to the Presbytery that the congregation in J. has called the Rev. T.

S., of the Presbytery of U., to become its pastor, and that he and Mr. Z. H., who is also present, have been appointed commissioners to prosecute the call.

The commissioners then placed the call in the hands of the Moderator, and requested leave to prosecute it before the Presbytery of U.

The call was found to be in order; and

Leave was granted to the commissioners to prosecute it before the Presbytery of U.

Mr. N. had leave of absence from the remaining sessions of the Presbytery.

The next stated meeting of the Presbytery was appointed to be holden in the Presbyterian church in A., on the fourth Tuesday in September next, at three o'clock, P.M.

The committee appointed to make arrangements for the installation of the Rev. D. O. as the pastor of the congregation in W., reported, recommending that the sermon be preached by the Rev. C. E.; that the Moderator preside, and "constitute the pastoral relation;" that the Rev. J. D. deliver the charge to the pastor, [or bishop,] and the Rev. A. B. the charge to the people; and that the concluding prayer be offered by the Rev. D. P.

The committee further recommends that, at the close of the present sessions, the Presbytery should adjourn, to meet in the Presbyterian church in W., on the 2d day of May next, at ten o'clock, A.M.*

The report of the committee was adopted.

The Presbytery then proceeded to the order of the day. The Statistical Reports of the Churches were read, and the Narratives of the State of Religion were given by the pastors and elders of the several churches.

The second order of the day was then taken up, and the Presbytery proceeded to the election of commissioners to represent the Presbytery in the next General Assembly.

The Rev. A. B., and Mr. J. R., elder, were duly elected the commissioners; and the Rev.

---

* When the person to be installed is already an ordained minister, and a member of the Presbytery with which the church is connected, if there is no other business to call for an adjourned meeting of the judicatory, it is usual to appoint the members, to whom the several parts of the service are assigned, a committee to perform the installation, in the name and on behalf of the Presbytery. This course is allowed in the "Form of Government," chap. xvi. sec. iv. Such a committee is often called a *commission*, because it is *empowered to act*, in the business assigned to it, *in the place* of the judicatory, and its report is made to inform the body *that the business is consummated;* whereas the report of a *committee* presents business arranged in proper order for the consideration and action of the judicatory. This distinction is presented here, because it is regarded by many as at once convenient and important.

D. P., and Mr. N. L., elder, were elected their alternates.

The roll of the churches under the care of the Presbytery was then called, and the amounts collected in the several congregations for the Commissioners' and Contingent Funds of the General Assembly were paid to the Treasurer.

The total amounts received were, $—— for the Commissioners' Fund, and $—— for the Contingent Fund:—and

The Treasurer was directed to forward the same to the Treasurer of the General Assembly.

The communication from the General Assembly's Committee of Publication, which had been put upon the docket, was taken up for consideration.

The communication was read, and

The following resolutions were unanimously adopted:—

Resolved, 1. That the Presbytery has heard with satisfaction the resolutions of the General Assembly with regard to the means for the promotion of the work intrusted to its Publication Committee.

Resolved, 2. That the session of each of the churches under our care be earnestly exhorted to take measures to carry out the recommendations of the Assembly.

Resolved, 3. That Messrs. D. B. and E. be a committee to ascertain the best mode of securing the circulation of the Committee's publications within our bounds, and that they report at the next stated meeting of Presbytery.

Messrs. D. and W., elders, had leave of absence from the remaining sessions of the Presbytery.

A recess was then taken until half-past one o'clock.

After the recess,

The committee to collect the tax for the incidental expenses of the Presbytery reported that he had received one dollar from each of the elders present: the total sum received being eight dollars.

The Treasurer was directed to obtain the tax from the church in D., which has not been represented in the present Sessions of the Presbytery.

The committees on the Records of the Sessions of C., E., R., W., and M., severally reported, recommending that they be approved, as far as written.

The reports were adopted.

The Rev. D. P. assigned the reasons why the

records of the Session of the church in A. had not been laid before the Presbytery during the present meeting.

The reasons were sustained.

The committee on the Records of the Session of B. reported, recommending that they be approved as far as written, with the following exceptions, namely:—

1. That the records are not signed, either by the Moderator or by the Clerk.

2. On pages 75 and 77, the Session appears to have adjourned, in both instances, without concluding their meeting with prayer.

3. On pages 79–81, in "recording the proceedings in a case of judicial process, the reasons for the decisions" made are not "recorded at length," as required by the "Book of Discipline," chapter iv. section xxiii.

The report was adopted.

The order of the day was postponed for the purpose of receiving a report from the Judicial Committee.

The report was in the words following, namely:—

The paper which was referred to the Judicial Committee purports to be a complaint against the Session of one of the churches under the care of the Presbytery, because of its refusing to commence a case of judicial process against an individual specified, on the ground of common fame.

The committee, having carefully considered the statements set forth in the paper, is clearly of the opinion that there is no ground of complaint against the Session, because, by the showing of the complainants themselves, the offence, if any, was strictly of a private nature, according to the "Book of Discipline," chapter ii. This will be evident on the reading of a brief extract from the paper.

The committee presents this extract only, since the reading of the whole paper would tend to give unnecessary publicity to the matters involved, and of the truth of which there is no evidence properly within the reach of the Presbytery.

In conclusion, the committee recommends the adoption of the following resolution:—

Resolved, That the said paper, purporting to be a complaint, be dismissed for the reason stated in the foregoing report.

The extract referred to by the committee was then read; and

The report was unanimously adopted.

The Presbytery then proceeded to the order of the day, namely:—the examination of candidates for licensure.

The Rev. A. B. introduced to the Presbytery Mr. J. G., a member of the church in E., and recommended him as a suitable person to be "taken on trials" as a "candidate for licensure."

The Presbytery proceeded to examine Mr. G. "respecting his experimental acquaintance with religion, and the motives which influence him to desire the sacred office."

The examination having proved satisfactory to the Presbytery, it was sustained, and

Mr. G. was "taken on trials" as a "candidate for licensure."

The Rev. Messrs. B. and P. were appointed a committee to recommend the subjects to be assigned to Mr. G. for his trial-pieces.

Mr. T. Y., a candidate under the care of the Presbytery, then made application for licensure at the present meeting.

Mr. Y. having completed the usual course of study in preparation for the ministry, and his examination in several departments of learning required by the "Form of Government," as well as the trial-pieces which he has presented, having at a former meeting of the Presbytery been sustained as "parts of trial,"

The Presbytery proceeded to examine him "on Theology, Natural and Revealed, and on

Ecclesiastical History, the Sacraments, and Church Government."*

The examination in each of these departments having been sustained,

Mr. Y. was directed to come this evening prepared to read his "popular sermon."

Messrs. S. H. and J. T. appeared in the Presbytery as commissioners from the congregation of P., in the Presbytery of D., deputed to prosecute a call to the Rev. R. F. to become their pastor.

The commissioners "produced a certificate from their own Presbytery, regularly attested by the Moderator and Clerk, that the call has been laid before them, and that it is in order," and requested leave to prosecute the same.

It having appeared that "the parties" are "not prepared to have the matter issued" at the present Sessions of the Presbytery, it was

Ordered, That the Stated Clerk address a written citation to the Rev. R. F. "and his congregation to appear before the Presbytery" at the adjourned meeting; and the Rev. C. E. was appointed to preach at M. on the next Sabbath, and to read the citation "from the

---

* The appointment, yearly, of examiners upon each department will greatly promote order, comfort, and thoroughness in the examination of candidates.

pulpit in that church," "immediately after public worship."*

The committee to which was referred the matter of arranging the order of supply for the pulpit of the church in R. reported the

---

[* If the call from a congregation in another Presbytery shall be addressed to a minister "without charge," the minute should be as in the text, through the second paragraph, and then proceed:—]

By the direction of the Presbytery, the call was placed in the hands of Mr. D. for consideration; and,

He having signified his disposition to accept it,

The following resolution was adopted, namely:—

Resolved, That the Rev. J. D., having accepted the call from the congregation of P., be, and he hereby is, dismissed from this Presbytery, and recommended to the Presbytery of D.; and he is hereby required "to repair to that Presbytery, that the proper steps may be taken for his regular settlement in that congregation."

[If such a call shall be addressed to a *licentiate*, the words "the Rev. R. F.," in the first paragraph of the minute of the text, should be replaced by the words "the licentiate D. R." Then, after the second paragraph, if the licentiate is present, proceed:—]

The Presbytery directed that the call should be placed in the hands of Mr. R. for his determination thereon; and,

He having signified his disposition to accept it,

The following resolution was adopted, namely:—

Resolved, That the licentiate D. R., having accepted the call from the congregation in P., be, and he hereby is, dismissed from the jurisdiction of this Presbytery, and recommended to that of the Presbytery of D.: and he is hereby following schedule, which was adopted, namely:—

SUPPLIES FOR THE PULPIT AT R——.

The Rev. Mr. D. to preach and administer the Lord's Supper in May; the Sabbath to be arranged by him after conference with the Session;

The Rev. Mr. F. to preach on the third Sabbath in June;

The Rev. Mr. B. to preach on the first Sabbath in July;

The Rev. Mr. O. to preach on the third Sabbath in July;

The Rev. Mr. J. to preach and administer the Lord's Supper on the second Sabbath in August;

The Rev. Mr. A. to preach on the fourth Sabbath in August; and

---

required "to repair to that Presbytery, and there to submit himself to the usual trials preparatory to ordination."

[If the person to whom the call is addressed, whether a minister without charge, or a licentiate, should not be present in the Presbytery, it will be necessary that he should be cited to attend the adjourned meeting; and the record, after the second paragraph in the text, should be:—]

The Rev. J. D. [or Mr. D. R.] not being present to answer the call,

The Stated Clerk was directed to cite him to appear before the Presbytery at the adjourned meeting.

The Rev. Mr. P. to preach on the second Sabbath in September.

The Moderator stated that only a very few items of business remained upon the docket, and suggested that, in the session of the Presbytery this evening, it would be peculiarly appropriate, both to the close of the sessions and to the nature of the matters yet to be attended to, if the transaction of the business should be alternated with devotional exercises.

The suggestion was cordially and unanimously adopted.

A recess was then taken until seven o'clock.

After the recess,

The committee appointed to nominate a preacher and to propose a subject for the discourse to be delivered on the Tuesday evening of the next stated meeting, reported, recommending that the Rev. C. E. be appointed the preacher, and that the Rev. D. P. be his alternate. The committee also proposed the following subject for the discourse, namely:—"The Priesthood of the Lord Jesus Christ."

The recommendations in this report were adopted.

The committee which was appointed to propose the subjects for the trial-pieces of the candidate J. G., made a report, recommending the following subjects, namely:—

1. *For a Latin Exegesis:—De Sanctificatione.*

2. *For a Critical Exercise:*—Romans viii. 19–23.

3. *For a Lecture:*—Galatians v. 22–25.

4. *For a Popular Sermon:*—Hebrews v. 9.

The report was adopted.

The committee which was appointed to prepare the Narrative of the State of Religion within the bounds of the Presbytery presented a report, which was adopted; and

The Stated Clerk was directed to transmit it, together with the Statistical Report of the Presbytery, to the next General Assembly.

The following is the

NARRATIVE.

[The Narrative may here be engrossed as a part of the minutes, or be put upon file, at the discretion of the Presbytery.]

Mr. Y., the candidate under examination, read his Popular Sermon, and it was sustained as a "part of trial."

The final vote was then taken, and it was

Resolved, That the Presbytery, having been well satisfied with the several "parts of trial" of the candidate T. Y., will now proceed to license him to preach the gospel "as a probationer for the holy ministry."

The candidate was then licensed in the manner and form prescribed in the "Form of Government," chapter xiv. sections vii. and viii.; and

The Stated Clerk was directed to furnish the licentiate T. Y. with the usual certificate of his licensure.

The transaction of business this evening was alternated with devotional exercises, under the direction of the Moderator, according to the previous agreement.

The minutes of the proceedings of to-day were read and approved.

After which,

The Presbytery adjourned, to meet in the Presbyterian church in W., on the 2d day of May next, at ten o'clock, A.M.

Concluded with prayer, singing the Doxology, and the benediction.

A. B., *Stated Clerk.*

Adjourned Meeting of the Presbytery.

The Presbytery met, pursuant to adjournment, in the Presbyterian church in W., on Wednesday, May 2d, 18—, at ten o'clock, A.M., and was opened with prayer by the Moderator, the Rev. B. J.

The following members were present, namely:—

MINISTERS.	CHURCHES.	ELDERS.

[The names are here to be inserted, as in the minutes of the stated meeting. The names of the absent members, also, and of the churches which are not represented, are to be recorded as at a stated meeting.]

So much of the minutes of the stated meeting as pertains to the several items of business which were laid over for the action of the Presbytery at this adjourned meeting was then read for the information of the judicatory.

After which,

The call of the congregation of P. to the Rev. R. F. to become its pastor, was taken up for consideration.

The Stated Clerk reported, that, according to the order adopted at the stated meeting, he had cited the Rev. R. F. "and his congregation to attend the present meeting," for the purpose of having the matter issued respecting his translation to the congregation of P., in the Presbytery of D.*

The Rev. C. E. reported that he had preached

* The "Form of Government," chap. xvi. sec. ii., directs that "at least two Sabbaths shall intervene betwixt the citation and the meeting of the Presbytery at which the cause of the translation is to be considered."

at M., according to the direction of the Presbytery, and had "read the citation from the pulpit in that church immediately after public worship."

Messrs. J. R. and L. B. appeared before the Presbytery as commissioners appointed by the congregation of M. to represent it in the matter of the proposed translation of its pastor.

The commissioners from the congregation of P. were also present.

By the direction of the Presbytery, the call from P. was placed in the hands of Mr. F. for his reply; and,

He having signified his disposition to accept it,

The commissioners from the congregation of M. were called upon to state whether that congregation "agrees to the translation" of the Rev. R. F. to the congregation of P.

Whereupon,

The commissioners from M. proceeded to state at length certain objections which that congregation had directed them to present for the consideration of the Presbytery.

The commissioners from the congregation of P. were also heard in the presentation of arguments in favor of the translation.

When they had concluded,

The hour for the public services of the

installation of the Rev. D. O. having arrived,

The further consideration of the call to Mr. F. was postponed until after the installation.

The Presbytery then proceeded to the installation of the Rev. D. O. as pastor of the congregation of W., and

The services were conducted according to the arrangement which was adopted at the stated meeting.

After the services,

The Presbytery resumed the transaction of business.

The call from the congregation of P. to the Rev. R. F. was then again taken up.

When all the parties had been fully heard,

The Presbytery, after careful deliberation,

Adopted the following resolutions, namely:—

Resolved, 1. That the pastoral relation heretofore existing between the Rev. R. F. and the congregation of M. be, and the same hereby is, dissolved, with a view to his accepting the call from the congregation of P.

Resolved, 2. That the Rev. R. F., having accepted the call from the congregation of P., be, and he hereby is, dismissed from this Presbytery, and recommended to the Presbytery of D.; and he is hereby required "to repair to that Presbytery, that the proper steps may be taken for his regular settlement in that congregation."

The Rev. J. D. was then appointed to preach at M., and, in the name of the Presbytery, to pronounce the pulpit vacant.

Mr. E. N., one of the commissioners to prosecute the call of the congregation in J. to the Rev. T. S. before the Presbytery of U., informed the Moderator that that Presbytery had placed the call in the hands of Mr. S., and that, he having signified his acceptance of the same, the Presbytery had dismissed him, and had required him "to repair to this Presbytery, that the proper steps may be taken for his regular settlement."

He then laid before the Presbytery "an authenticated certificate" of these transactions, "under the hand of the Clerk" of the Presbytery of U., which was read, and

Mr. S. was received as a member of this Presbytery.

The commissioner from J. then informed the Moderator that it is the desire of the congregation that the installation may take place on ——, the —— day of —— next, at two o'clock, P.M.

Whereupon, it was

Resolved, That when the Presbytery shall

adjourn, it will adjourn to meet in the Presbyterian church in J. on ——, the —— day of —— next, at one o'clock, P.M.

The minutes of the proceedings of this adjourned meeting were read and approved.

After which,

The Presbytery adjourned, to meet in the Presbyterian church in J. on ——, the —— day of —— next, at one o'clock, P.M.

Concluded with prayer and the benediction.

A. B., *Stated Clerk.*

[The adjournment of an *adjourned* meeting should be in the same form as that of a stated meeting, except that generally the singing at the close may be omitted. If there is to be no adjourned meeting before the time of the next stated meeting, the adjournment, whether of a stated or of an adjourned meeting, should always be to the place and time of the next stated meeting.]

A Special Meeting of the Presbytery.

The Presbytery met in the Presbyterian church in B. on Thursday, February 15th, 18—, at eleven o'clock, A.M., pursuant to the call of the Moderator, the Rev. A. B., and was opened with prayer.

The call of the Moderator was then read, and is as follows:—

CIRCULAR LETTER.

[Here insert the Moderator's letter in full.]

The following members were present, namely:—

MINISTERS.	CHURCHES.	ELDERS.

[The names are to be inserted here, as in the minutes of the stated meeting. The names of the members who are absent, and of the churches which are not represented, are also to be recorded.]

The Presbytery proceeded to the transaction of the business for which it had been convened.

The Rev. C. M. requested leave to resign the pastoral charge of the congregation in R., and assigned the reasons which have induced him to make this request.

Messrs. B. D. and G. R. appeared before the Presbytery as commissioners from the congregation at R., and stated that a meeting of the congregation had been holden, at which it had been determined to offer no obstruction to the granting of the request of the pastor, although it would be greatly to the satisfaction of the people to have him remain among them as heretofore.

The reasons presented by Mr. M. for his request were then deliberately considered; and it was

Resolved, That his request be granted, and that the pastoral relation which has existed between him and the congregation at R. be, and the same hereby is, dissolved from this day.

The Rev. D. P. was appointed to preach at R., and, in the name of the Presbytery, to pronounce the pulpit vacant.

The Rev. C. M. then requested a dismission from this Presbytery, and a recommendation to the Presbytery of N., into the bounds of which he expects shortly to remove.

His request was granted.

Mr. J. N., a licentiate under the care of the Presbytery of B., presented a certificate of dismission and recommendation from that body, and requested to be taken under the care of this Presbytery.

The certificate having been found to be in order,

His request was granted.

A joint application was then received from the licentiate J. N., and the Session of the church in J., requesting the Presbytery to proceed to ordain him, the said licentiate, as an evangelist, with a view to his taking charge of the congregation at J. as its stated supply.

Mr. E. N., the elder representing the Session of J., made a statement of the situation and prospects of that congregation, and of the reasons which had induced the Session to join in the present application.

Whereupon,

After a protracted investigation of all the circumstances of the case as the same are now before the judicatory,

It was unanimously *Resolved*,

1. That while the Presbytery is disposed to grant, so far as it consistently can, every request of the Session of the church in J., and while it has great confidence in the wisdom and prudence of the said Session, and also in the character of Mr. N.,—so far as it has enjoyed the opportunity of becoming acquainted with him,—it is yet, by a careful examination of the whole matter, constrained to decide that the way does not appear to be prepared to proceed to the ordination of the said licentiate, J. N., at this time.

2. That the further consideration of the joint application be postponed until the stated meeting.

The minutes of the proceedings of this special meeting were read and approved.

The Presbytery then adjourned.

Concluded with prayer and the benediction.

A. B., *Stated Clerk.*

NOTE.—*Respecting the Dismission of a Pastor.*

In the minutes of the stated and adjourned meetings the subject of the dismission of a pastor has been treated in exact accordance with the provisions of the "Form of Government."

In the minutes of the special meeting we have introduced the matter in conformity with what is now the more general custom. When a minister has decided to leave his congregation for some other field of labor, it is customary for him to call a meeting of the congregation, and to request it to unite with him in requesting the Presbytery to dissolve the pastoral relation. Of this meeting and its action report is made by its commissioners to the Presbytery, and that body then proceeds to act upon the application without delay.

That this custom has its advantages, is not denied; chief among which are:—1. The saving of time to the Presbytery; which, according to the method in the "Book," must hold an adjourned meeting, having, it may be, *this request* as its only business; and, 2. Abbreviating, possibly, the period during which a congregation may be held in suspense, if not in anxiety, on the subject of its pastor's resignation.

But it is a serious question, whether this

compendious method may not have been productive of evil quite as much as of good:—whether, by reason of the facility with which it disposes of the pastoral tie, it may not have exerted a real and not inconsiderable influence in rendering the connection so unstable, that in many sections of the Church the office of pastor has fallen into disuse to an alarming degree. Other causes have, indeed, existed; causes which, in many instances, have been more obvious. Still, the inquiry is submitted, whether many pastors have not been dismissed because it was *so easy* to dissolve the relation, who, had the mode prescribed in the "Book" been the only one by which they could have disengaged themselves, would have remained at the post of duty, and lived down and labored down the difficulties which for a season might have disturbed their peace.

Application to the Moderator for the Calling of a Special Meeting of the Presbytery.

To the Rev. A. B.,

Moderator of the Presbytery of H.

Rev. and Dear Sir:—

In accordance with the provisions of the "Form of Government," chap. x. sec. x., you are hereby requested to call a special meeting of the said Presbytery, to be holden in the Presbyterian church in B., on Thursday, the 15th day of February next, at eleven o'clock, A.M., for the purpose of considering, and—if the way shall be prepared—of issuing, the following matters of business, namely:—

I. An application from the Rev. C. M. for leave to resign the pastoral charge of the congregation in R., together with the action of the said congregation thereupon.

II. The request of the Rev. Mr. M. for a dismission from this Presbytery, and a recommendation to the Presbytery of N.

III. An application from Mr. J. N., a licentiate of the Presbytery of B., to be received under the care of this Presbytery.

IV. The joint application of Mr. N. and the session of the church in J., requesting the Presbytery to ordain him as an evangelist,—if the way shall be prepared,—with a view to his taking charge of said church, as its stated supply.

We are, Rev. and dear sir,
Very respectfully,
Your brethren and friends,

(Signed) R. A.
D. P.
J. H., Elder of the Church in J.
W. T., Elder of the Church in B.

January 29, 18—.

The Moderator's Letter, calling a Special Meeting of the Presbytery.

CIRCULAR LETTER.

B——, January 31, 18—.

Application having been made to me, in accordance with the provisions of the "Form of Government," chap. x. sec. x., a special meeting of the Presbytery of H. will be holden, (D. V.,) in the Presbyterian church in B., on Thursday, the 15th day of February next, at eleven o'clock, A.M., for the purpose of considering, and—if the way shall be prepared—of issuing, the following matters of business, namely:—

[Here specify distinctly every item of the business which is to be presented for the action of the Presbytery, as in the foregoing application to the Moderator.]

(Signed) A. B., *Moderator.*

[Annexed to the circular should be the following invitations:—

To a Pastor, or a Stated Supply.]

To the Rev. R. A.

REV. AND DEAR BROTHER:—

You are hereby notified of the special meeting of the Presbytery of H.,—as above called,—and requested to attend the same, accompanied by the representative of the Session of the church in C.

Yours, fraternally,

A. B., *Moderator.*

B——, January 31, 18—.

[To the Session of a Vacant Church.]

To the Session of the Church in J.

DEAR BRETHREN :—

You are hereby notified of the special meeting of the Presbytery of H.,—as above called,—and requested to attend the same, by your representative.

Yours, fraternally,

A. B., *Moderator.*

B——, January 31, 18—.

Organization of a Church.

[When a number of individuals, with their families, desire to be formed into a church, after full consultation and agreement among themselves, they should send a delegation, of two or more of their number, to apply to the Presbytery, within whose bounds they reside, for direction and counsel in effecting their organization. Of this application of the delegates, and of the action of the Presbytery thereupon, the following record may be made in the minutes :—]

Messrs. B. A. and J. C. appeared before the Presbytery as a delegation from a number of individuals residing in O., who desire to be organized, with their families, into a Presbyterian church in connection with this Presbytery, and requested that all the measures necessary to effect this object may be taken by the Presbytery without unnecessary delay.

The delegates were then heard in an extended statement respecting the number and circumstances of the applicants, and the prospective support and increase of a Presbyterian church in O. and its vicinity.

After a free conversation with the delegates,—and

In view of all the information that was elicited,—

The Presbytery appointed a commission, consisting of the Rev. Messrs. A. B. and C. D., and Mr. E. F., elder, to meet at O., on Tuesday, the —— day of —— next, at two o'clock, P.M., to confer with the applicants, and with others interested, and to make all necessary investigations, and—if the way shall be prepared—to proceed to the organization of a Presbyterian church, according to the request to that effect which has been presented by the delegation.

The delegates from O. were requested to make all the arrangements for the meeting of the commission which may be necessary; and, particularly, to represent to the applicants the great importance of obtaining immediately, from the churches with which they are severally connected, certificates of dismission, recommending them to the Presbyterian church about to be organized.

[At the time appointed, the commission should seek all the information necessary to a judicious decision of the question intrusted to it. If the way shall seem to be prepared for organizing a church at that time, the commission should proceed to receive the certificates of the applicants, and to examine such as may desire to make, on this occasion, their public profession of religion.

The names of all whose certificates, or examination, are approved, having been enrolled, a private meeting should be holden in some suitable place, at which the commission may confer freely with the applicants, giving them such advice as their circumstances may seem to require; proposing to them a form of a confession of faith and covenant for the adoption and use of the church to be organized; and making all necessary arrangements for the public services of the organization of the church. At this private meeting the ruling elders and deacons should be informally chosen, so that there may be no delay at the public services. It should also be arranged that all the persons to be received into the new church shall be *seated together* at the organization service.

When the time for the public services shall have arrived, it is proper that one of the members of the commission should preach a sermon adapted to the occasion. After which, the chairman should state to the audience the several steps which have been taken, and the nature of the duty about to be performed. He should then read from the register the names of the persons who are to be organized into a church, mentioning the church by which each one has been recommended, and indicating those who are to be received on the profession of their faith. Then, calling upon the whole company to arise, he should read to them the Confession of Faith, requiring from each individual some distinct token of adoption,—either by the voice, or by raising the hand, or by an inclination of the head. If any of the new professors are to be baptized, that sacrament should now be administered. The chairman should then read the covenant, and, all having given their assent thereto, as before to the Confession, he should solemnly address himself to the company, in the following, or like words,—his colleagues now standing by his side:—]

Having received from you this confession of your faith, and your public assent to this covenant, we, constituting the commission of the Presbytery of H., and for this purpose representing it here, do, in the name and on behalf of the said Presbytery, and in the name and by the authority of the Lord Jesus Christ, the ever-living Head of the Church on earth and in heaven, pronounce and declare that you are this day regularly organized and established as the First Presbyterian Church in O., in accordance with the order of the Presbyterian Church in these United States:—and may the blessing of Almighty God, the Father, the Son, and the Holy Ghost, descend upon and abide with you and your children from this day forth, to establish and strengthen you, to comfort and guide you, and to conduct you at last to the General Assembly and Church of the First-born, in his own glorious temple in heaven! Amen.

[The members of the new church being again seated, the chairman should say,—]

The following persons, having been *informally* chosen to the offices of ruling elder and deacon in this church, are now to be considered as properly nominated for election by the church, if so it shall please. Listen to their names:—Messrs. B. A., D. C., and F. E., for the office of ruling elder; and Messrs. H. G. and J. I., for the office of deacon.

If it is now your free will and desire that these brethren, being, according to the rule of our Church, "all male members in full communion" in the First Presbyterian Church in O., shall be elected to the offices in this church to which they have been nominated, you will please to "hold up the right hand in testimony of assent."

[After having received the affirmative vote, the chairman should proceed to say,—]

On the other hand, if there are any who dissent from this election, let such indicate it by the same sign.

[The vote having been declared, let the elders elect be called forth before the assembly, and let the questions prescribed in the "Form of Government," chap. xiii. sec. iv., be put to them and to the church. In the same manner let the deacons elect be called forth,—the elders still continuing to stand,—and, the appointed questions having been put and answered affirmatively, let the new officers be solemnly set apart to their respective offices by prayer and the laying on of hands.

If either of the elders or deacons has formerly been ordained to the office to which he is now elected in the new church, only the fourth and fifth of the prescribed questions should be proposed to him, inasmuch as to him the service is not ordination, but only installation into that particular charge.

The church having now been organized, and its officers ordained and installed, an affectionate charge and exhortation should be addressed to it by one of the members of the commission; after which, let it, with all its interests, be solemnly commended to God in prayer.

It will be very appropriate, if time and other circumstances will permit, for the commission, after a recess, if required on account of the length of the preceding services, to administer to the new church the sacrament of the Lord's Supper. But if this may not be done by the commission, the elders should make arrangements for the celebration of that sacrament on the earliest Sabbath on which they can secure the presence of one of the ministers of the Presbytery.

At the next meeting of the Presbytery the commission should present a report of its doings, of which, unless it shall be deemed important to prepare a more extended report, the following notice may be taken in the minutes:—]

The commission which was appointed at the last stated meeting to organize a church in our connection at O., if the way should be prepared, reported that it had performed the duty assigned to it; that the new church had been organized with —— members, of whom —— were received on certificates from other churches, and —— on the profession of their faith; and that three ruling elders and two deacons had been elected and ordained, or installed; of whom Mr. A. B. is now present as the representative of that Session.

The report of the commission was accepted.

Mr. B. A., a ruling elder from the church in O., then requested that the church which he represents should be taken under the care of this Presbytery; and that, as its representative, he may be recognised in the present sessions.

Whereupon, it was

Resolved, 1. That the First Presbyterian Church in O. be, and it hereby is, received under the care of this Presbytery, according to its request, and that its name be now entered upon the roll of our churches.

2. That Mr. B. A., a ruling elder in the First Presbyterian Church in O., be received as its representative; and that, as such, he is entitled to a seat in this house as a member of this judicatory.

Discipline.

[It does not pertain to the scope of the present work to discuss the various questions that have arisen in regard to the manner in which offences are to be brought to the cognizance of a Judicatory,—whether by an individual accuser, or on the ground of "general rumor" or "common fame." Our "Book of Discipline" allows of both modes, and is sufficiently discriminating in regard to the circumstances in which each is appropriate. It is our duty, therefore, to furnish the necessary "forms" required by the "Process" according to each mode.

It is hardly necessary to remark that, the principles of our "Discipline" being the same whatever the Judicatory before which the "Process" is conducted, the "forms" which we shall give are equally applicable, *mutatis mutandis*, to the Session and to the Presbytery.

We begin with a case before *the Session*, and of a kind to be recognized on the ground of

"Common Fame."

The first notice of the case may appear upon the records in the following form, namely:—]

The Session, having been informed that rumors are in circulation seriously affecting the Christian reputation of one of the members of this church, appointed Mr. B. a committee to investigate the matter, and, if he shall find "probable ground of accusation," to prepare the charge in proper form, and to report at the next meeting.

[The name of the offender is not mentioned in this minute, for prudential reasons. If the rumor is so clamorous as to make it necessary to insert the name in the first notice of the case, the phrase "one of the members" may be replaced by "J. B. G., a member," &c. But it is better, if possible, to suppress the name until it shall have become evident that a judicial investigation cannot be avoided.

At the next meeting, if the committee shall report that he is satisfied that the rumors are without foundation, the record may be made in the words following, namely:—]

The committee appointed at the last meeting of the Session to investigate the rumors concerning one of the members of this church, reported that he has discharged the duty assigned to him, and is satisfied that the reports affecting the reputation of our Christian brother are altogether without foundation in truth, and had their origin in the personal malice of an unworthy individual.

This report having been sustained, by a statement of facts, to the satisfaction of the Session, it was

Resolved, That the report be accepted, and that no further notice be taken of the matter.

[If the committee believes the rumors to be true, but not susceptible of clear and decisive proof at present, the record should be:—]

The committee appointed at the last meeting of the Session to investigate the rumors concerning one of them embers of this church, reported that he has discharged the duty assigned to him, and is satisfied that the reports affecting the Christian reputation of the individual in question are well founded. At the same time, he is convinced that the offence, in the language of the "Book of Discipline," chap. iii. sec. iii., is "so circumstanced that it plainly cannot be prosecuted to conviction" by any testimony at present within the command of the Session.

This report having been sustained, by a statement of facts, to the satisfaction of the Session,

It was *Resolved*,

1. That the report of the committee be accepted.

2. That it appears to be evident that the case is one of the class intended in the section of the "Book of Discipline" referred to by the committee; and that, "however grievous it may be to the pious to see an unworthy member in the church, it is proper to wait until God, in his righteous providence, shall give further light."

[If at a subsequent time it shall appear that "sufficient proof" of the offence can be obtained, a case disposed of as in the preceding minute may be reopened in the following form:—]

The Session, having been informed that the rumors affecting the Christian reputation of the member of this church, referred to in the minutes on pages 69, 70, and 71 of these records, continue still to circulate to the injury of religion, and that "sufficient proof" of the offence can now be obtained, appointed Mr. B. a committee to re-investigate the matter, and, if he shall find "probable ground of accusation," to prepare the charge in proper form, and to report at the next meeting of the Session.

[If the committee shall be convinced that the case is one requiring the immediate exercise of discipline, the following form should be adopted for the minute, namely :—]

The committee appointed at the last meeting of the Session to investigate [or, to re-investigate] the rumors concerning one of the members of this church, reported that, in the discharge of the duty assigned to him, it became apparent that the case is one which requires the interposition of the Session; that he is satisfied that there is "probable ground of accusation;" and that, in obedience to the order of the Session, he has prepared the following

CHARGE.

Common fame charges J. B. G., a member of this church, with *the sin of intemperance*, to the manifest injury of his own Christian standing and reputation, and to the flagrant reproach of the Church of Christ,—as set forth in the following specifications, namely :—

Specification First.

In this, that, on or about the 15th day of the month of April last, at the time of the auction-sale on the premises of D. C., the said J. B. G., then being present at the said auction, did so conduct himself as to attract the attention and remark of many individuals, and, by his boisterous and silly conversation and unseemly actions, did lead the bystanders to believe that he was under the influence and control of intoxicating liquor; the more especially as he was seen in several instances to indulge in drinking liquors of this description.

Specification Second.

In this, that, on or about the 1st day of the month of May last, the said J. B. G., then being at the public house of J. R., in this town, did frequently indulge in drinking intoxicating liquors, and did exhibit various symptoms of his having drank to excess.

Specification Third.

In this, that, on or about the 10th day of the month of June last, the said J. B. G., then being upon the public highway between the public house of J. R. aforesaid and his own dwelling, and going in the direction towards the latter place, when near the house of R. S., was seen to stagger in his walk, and in other respects to make it evident that he was under the influence and control of intoxicating liquors.

Specification Fourth.

In this, that, on or about the 4th day of the month of July last, the said J. B. G., then being upon the public square in this village, during the time of the Annual Celebration of "Independence Day," was seen to exhibit many tokens of his being in a state of intoxication, particularly in his gait, in the indecent exposure of his person, in the foul and abusive language with which he replied to one who kindly expostulated with him in regard to his condition and deportment, and in his efforts to inflict bodily injury upon certain individuals who made a friendly attempt to withdraw him from public observation.'

The foregoing charge, with its specifications, may be proved by the testimony of the following witnesses, namely:*—

---

* If it is preferred, the names of the witnesses may be attached to each specification. When there are two or more *charges*, it is better that the witnesses relied upon to prove each separate charge should be named at the close of the specifications under that charge.

Mr. B. A.	Mrs. E. S.
" D. C.	" C. R.
" F. E.	Miss H. S.
" R. S.	Mr. C. H.
" T. W.	" G. T.

Mr. W. R.

The report of the committee was accepted;

And it was *Resolved*,

1. That the Session will proceed without delay to a judicial investigation of the case as presented in the charge and specifications reported by the committee.

2. That when the Session shall adjourn, it will adjourn to meet in the lecture-room, on Tuesday, the —— day of —— inst., at two o'clock, P.M.; and

The clerk was directed to cite the accused to appear before the Session, at that time and place.

Mr. B. was appointed the "Committee of Prosecution," to "conduct the whole cause on the part of the prosecution."

[The "Book of Discipline" directs that "no more shall be done at the first meeting, unless by consent of parties, than to give the accused a copy of each charge, with the names of the witnesses to support it; and to cite all concerned to appear at the next meeting, &c."

If the accused person is present at the meeting at which the accusation is allowed, a copy of the charges may be "given" to him, and all the parties may be cited, as in the case before a

Presbytery, hereafter presented. (See p. 86.) But if he is absent, as is generally the case when a private member of the church is accused before the Session, it seems to be required by the "Book" that a "*first meeting*" should be had, at which the accused may come before the Judicatory, and be furnished with the charges, &c., prior to the one at which he and the witnesses are to appear, for the purpose of proceeding to the trial.

Attention to this matter would prevent the summoning of the witnesses to attend a meeting at which they cannot be examined, unless the accused shall consent to waive his privilege of delay, and to proceed at once to the trial,—a waiver which the Judicatory has no right to anticipate. It would also prove the means of saving much time, which in so many cases is consumed, at the commencement of "actual process," in the discussion of this very question—which is to be considered as the "first meeting," as intended by the "Book."

At the "first meeting," as appointed in the preceding minutes, if the accused person is present, let the following record be made:—]

The unfinished business of the last meeting, namely, The charge which was tabled, on the ground of common fame, against J. B. G., a member of this church, was taken up, and, Mr. G. being present, "a copy of the charge" and its specifications, "with the names of the witnesses to support it," was given to him.

Mr. G. requested that Mr. H., one of the members of this Session, may be assigned to him as counsel, to aid him in the preparation and exhibition of his defence.

The request was granted; and Mr. H. was accordingly appointed to that service.*

It was then *Ordered*,

1. That "all concerned" be cited "to appear at the next meeting" of the Session, "to have the matter fully heard and decided."

2. That when the Session shall adjourn, it will adjourn to meet in this place, on Tuesday, the —— day of ——, at two o'clock, P.M.

3. That the clerk issue written citations to the accused party, and to the witnesses named in the charge against him, to appear before the Session at the time and place appointed in the preceding order; and that he also furnish the accused with citations for such witnesses as he may desire to summon to testify in his behalf.

At the adjourned meeting, after the routine business is completed, let the record proceed:—]

It having been ascertained that the citations ordered at the last meeting "have been duly

---

* Although the language of the "Book of Discipline," chap. iv. sec. xxi., implies that an accused person may, even without obtaining the consent of the Judicatory, request one of its members to act as his counsel, yet custom and a decent respect for the Judicatory require that the appointment should be requested as in the text.

served on the persons for whom they were intended," and

Mr. J. B. G., the accused person, and Mr. B., the "Committee of Prosecution," being present, and

Both parties having declared that they were ready for trial,

The Session proceeded to the investigation of the "business assigned for trial."

The Moderator "solemnly announced from the chair, that the body is about to pass to the consideration of the business assigned for trial; and enjoined on the members to recollect and regard their high character, as judges of a court of Jesus Christ, and the solemn duty in which they are about to act."

The charge, with its specifications, as recorded on page 69 of these minutes, was then read to the accused party, and

He was "called upon to say whether he is guilty or not" of the things charged against him.

Whereupon

The accused made answer, "I am not guilty."

The "Committee of Prosecution" then addressed the Judicatory, presenting his view of the case committed to him, and stating the points which he expects to prove by the witnesses, whose names are annexed to the charge and specifications.*

After which

He proceeded to call the witnesses.

The Moderator now stated that, according to the "Book of Discipline," chapter vi. section vii., "No witness afterward to be examined, except a member of the Judicatory, shall be present during the examination of another witness on the same case, unless by consent of parties."

Mr. H., the counsel for the accused, insisted on the exclusion of the witnesses, according to the rule; and

It was *Ordered* accordingly.

Mr. B. then introduced the first witness for the prosecution,

Mr. B. A., who was sworn by the Moderator, and testified as follows:—

[According to section xvii. of the chapter "Of Witnesses," "the testimony given by witnesses must be faithfully recorded, and read to them, for their approbation or subscription;" and, according to section x. of the same chapter, "every question

---

* As the "Book of Discipline" does not prescribe the form of proceeding in its details, it must be left to the judgment of the Committee of Prosecution, under leave of the Judicatory, whether he will "open" the case by a statement of what he expects to prove, or proceed at once to the examination of the witnesses.

put to a witness shall, if required, be reduced to writing. When answered, it shall, together with the answer, be recorded, if deemed by either party of sufficient importance."

The testimony may be entered upon the records with the minutes, or, as is more frequently done, it may be recorded separately, and be preserved "on file."

At the close of the testimony of each witness, it should be distinctly stated that]

The testimony was read to the witness, and approved by him as being correctly recorded.

[When all the testimony, for the prosecution and for the defence, shall have been received, the record should proceed, as follows:—]

The witnesses having all been examined,

The parties were heard in their explanations of the testimony, and in their comments upon it.

After they had concluded, and had withdrawn from the house,*

The roll was called, that every member of the Judicatory might "have an opportunity to express his opinion on the case."

After which,

The final vote was taken, and

---

* Although there is no express rule which requires that the parties in an original trial shall withdraw from the house at this stage of the proceedings, the principle is the same, and the necessity quite as imperative, as in the case of an appeal, in which the "Book" expressly requires all parties to withdraw.

The charge, with its specifications, was holden to be proved.

Whereupon

The following minute was unanimously adopted:—

The Session, having deliberately considered the testimony in the case of J. B. G., a member of this church, charged by common fame with the *sin of intemperance*, as in sundry specifications set forth, and having patiently listened to the arguments and explanations which have been offered, as well by the accused as by the Committee of Prosecution, does judge and decide that the charge has been proved, and that the said J. B. G. is guilty of the *sin of intemperance* charged upon him.

And the Session does further judge and determine that the said J. B. G. ought to be, and he hereby is, suspended from the communion of the church, until he shall give satisfactory evidence of repentance.

Mr. G. was then called in, and

The Moderator, in accordance with the "Directory for Worship," chapter x. section iii., pronounced upon him the sentence of the Judicatory.

After which,

Mr. G. gave notice of his intention to appeal from this decision of the Session to the Presbytery of H. at its next meeting, and stated that a copy of his appeal, with the reasons for the same, should be "lodged with the Moderator" "within ten days."*

The following minute was then adopted:—

In view of the publicity of the offence of which J. B. G., one of the members of this church, has been proved to be guilty, and of the great reproach which has been brought by it upon the Church of Christ,

The Session judges, that fidelity to the interests of religion renders it highly proper and important that the above sentence should be made public; and

The Moderator was requested to publish the same from the pulpit.

[The "Book of Discipline," chap. iv. sec. ix., seems to contemplate a class of offences in which more private means may be resorted to for removing the scandal. This class may consist of offences of less heinous character, or of such as, while they are less extensively known, still do not properly come under the designation of "*private* offences."

---

* This notice of an appeal is inserted for the purpose of exhibiting the proper form for the minute, and the appropriate time for giving the notice; although in a case like the one supposed there is little probability of an appeal being taken. If an appeal *is* taken, the minute which follows in the text ought not to be adopted until the appeal shall have been decided in favor of the Judicatory. See "Book of Discipline," chap. vii. sec. iii. sub-sec. xv.

The first notice of such a case may appear on the records, as follows:—]

The Session, from information which it has received, having reason to fear that one of the members of the church has exhibited conduct unbecoming the Christian profession, appointed Mr. D. a committee to visit him for the purpose of conversing with him "in a private manner," and of "endeavoring to bring him to repentance."

[At the next meeting, the report of the committee, if he has been successful, may be recorded in the following manner:—]

Mr. D. reported that he has visited the brother to whom he was sent by the Session, and has had free conversation with him in reference to the matter in question; that he acknowledged the report which the Session has heard to be true; that he appeared to be sincerely penitent in view of the injury which his conduct has brought upon the Christian name; and that he declared his purpose, by the grace of God, to avoid in future whatever may be inconsistent with a "conversation as it becometh the gospel of Christ."

The report was accepted; and it was

Resolved, That no further notice be taken of the matter.

[If the committee shall not be successful in these private efforts, the report should be:—]

Mr. D. reported that he has visited the brother to whom he was sent by the Session, and has conversed privately with him in reference to the matter in question, but has entirely failed of obtaining any satisfactory result. He further reported that he is convinced that the case is one which requires judicial investigation, and that he is satisfied that there is "probable ground of accusation."

The report was accepted; and,

After full deliberation,

Mr. D. was directed to prepare the charge in proper form, and to report the same at the next meeting of the Session.

[At the next meeting the report of the committee should be entered upon the records, as follows:—]

Mr. D. reported that, having made further efforts, in the case of the brother to whom he was sent, to bring him to repentance, and having altogether failed of success, in obedience to the order of the Session at its last meeting, he has prepared the charge against him in the following form, namely:—

CHARGE.

Common fame charges P. J., a member of this church, with *unworthy and unchristian con-*

duct, as the same is set forth in the following specifications:—

Specification First.

In this, that the said P. J. has been guilty of *breaking a matrimonial engagement;* that is to say: In the month of May last, on or about the 25th day of the month, he entered into a voluntary engagement of marriage with Miss E. R., of H., which engagement being still undischarged he has violated and broken, by becoming the married husband of another woman.

Specification Second.

In this, that the said P. J. has been guilty of *duplicity in his intercourse* with Miss E. R. aforesaid; that is to say: Pending the engagement, as declared in Specification First, and while Miss R. was led, by his conversation and letters, to place full reliance in his promise of marriage, and to make preparation, on her part, for the solemnization of their marriage, he did, notwithstanding, engage to marry, and did actually marry, another woman, as stated in Specification First.

Specification Third.

In this, that the said P. J. has been guilty of *wilful falsehood*; that is to say: Pending the engagement, as declared in Specification

First, and while the said engagement was freely and repeatedly acknowledged by him, not only to Miss R. herself, but also to her family and friends, he did, notwithstanding, at sundry times, and particularly on or about the 2d day of June last, and again on or about the 15th day of the same month of June, deliberately and solemnly deny, to one or more individuals, that any such engagement did exist, or had existed, between himself and Miss R., or any other woman.

Which charge, with its specifications, may be proved by the testimony of the following witnesses and letters, namely:—

Mr. J. H. R.	Miss E. R.
" A. D. G.	" C. H. L.
" R. W.	" L. L. E.

Mr. J.'s letter to Miss R., dated at E., June 6, 18–
" " " " " " " " " " 12, "
" " " " Mr. L. J. B., " " " 15, "

The report of the committee was accepted.

[Then proceed as in the former case.]

[We come now to present the "forms" for a case in which there is

An Individual Accuser;

and we shall suppose it to be brought before a *Presbytery*, repeating the remark before made, that, with the circumstantial alterations necessary, the "forms" will be appropriate also to a similar case before a Session.

The individual bringing the accusation should present it in writing, addressed to the Moderator of the Presbytery; and the record should be as follows:—]

The Moderator informed the Presbytery that he has received a communication from the Rev. G. T., a member of this Presbytery, [or, a member of the Presbytery of J.; or, from Mr. G. T., a member of the church in B., under the care of this Presbytery,] accompanied by a request that it may be laid before the Judicatory, for its consideration.

The paper was then read; and,

After full deliberation, it was

Ordered, That it be entered upon the minutes.

The following is the communication:—

A——, January 1, 18—.

To the Rev. A. B.,

Moderator of the Presbytery of H.

REV. AND DEAR SIR:—

Permit me to request that you will lay before the Presbytery over which you preside, the following paper, for its consideration, and for such action in the premises as the merits of the case may require.

It has become my painful duty to lay upon the table of the Presbytery the accompanying charges affecting the Christian and ministerial standing of one of the members of this body. This is not a hasty procedure. I have endeavored, in the manner prescribed by our Lord in the eighteenth chapter of Matthew, to bring this offending brother to repentance. But I have utterly failed; and I find no reason to hope that by further delay, or by a renewal of private efforts, any good end will be accomplished. In this feeling the two brethren, whom I took with me in the second stage of this process, fully concur. In their opinion, as well as in my own, I have no choice but to invoke the interposition of the Presbytery; and I, therefore, respectfully ask leave to prosecute before this Judicatory the following

CHARGE.

The Rev. G. T. charges the Rev. P. B., a member of this Presbytery, with *unchristian and unministerial conduct*, as set forth in the following specifications, namely:—

Specification First.

[Here insert the specifications, and append the names of all the witnesses, after the models already given; and then conclude as follows:—]

All of which is respectfully submitted.
(Signed)
G. T., a member of the Presbytery of H.; [or, a member of the Presbytery of J.; or, G. T., a member of the church in B., under the care of the Presbytery of H.]

Mr. T. was "warned that," according to the "Book of Discipline," chap. v. section vii., "if he fails to prove the charge, he must himself be censured as a slanderer of the gospel ministry, in proportion to the malignancy or rashness that shall appear in the prosecution."

To which warning he returned the following written reply:—

The Rev. G. T. replies, and declares that, so far as he is able to judge his own motives, he has been induced to enter upon the present course of discipline solely by an imperative sense of duty; and he cheerfully assents to the propriety of the rule which has been read to him, and promises to submit himself to the just censure of the Presbytery, if he shall exhibit either "malignancy or rashness in the prosecution."

Leave was then granted to him to prosecute the charge, with its specifications, as above recorded.

Whereupon, Mr. B., the minister accused, being present, "a full copy of the charges, with the names of the witnesses annexed," was given to him.

Mr. B. requested that the Rev. C. E., a member of the Presbytery, may be assigned to him as counsel, to aid him in the preparation and exhibition of his defence from the charge which has been tabled against him.

The request was granted, and the Rev. C. E. consenting, he was appointed counsel for the accused.

It was then *Ordered*,

1. That the "parties and their witnesses" be cited "to appear and be heard at the next meeting."

2. That, when the Presbytery shall adjourn, it will adjourn to meet in this place, [or, at ——,] on Tuesday, the —— day of ——, at eleven o'clock, A.M.

3. That the Stated Clerk issue written citations to the parties and to the witnesses above named, to appear before the Presbytery at the time and place appointed in the preceding order; and that he also furnish the accused with citations for such witnesses as he may desire to summon to testify in his behalf.

[The subsequent proceedings will differ so little from those exhibited in the first case before the Session, that it is not deemed necessary to carry out the present trial any further,—except to furnish appropriate "forms" for the "Finding" of the Judicatory in a case of an "Individual Accuser."

If the "Finding" is that the charge has been proved, the record may be made in the following terms:—]

The Presbytery of H., having heard the charge against the Rev. P. B., presented by the

Rev. G. T., having carefully examined all the testimony introduced by both the parties, and having patiently considered the arguments and explanations which have been offered, as well by the accused as by the prosecutor, is constrained to decide that the charge against the said Rev. P. B. has been fully proved. And, further,

The Presbytery, having deliberately considered the whole case, does unanimously judge and determine, that the said Rev. P. B. ought to be, and he hereby is, suspended from the exercise of the functions, all and singular, of his office, as a minister of the gospel, until he shall give satisfactory evidence of repentance.

[If the Judicatory shall decide that the charge has *not* been proved, it may be necessary to rebuke the prosecutor, according to the warning given to him at the beginning, for the temper in which he has conducted the prosecution; in which case the record should be :—]

The Presbytery of H., having heard the charge against the Rev. P. B. preferred by the Rev. G. T., having carefully examined all the testimony introduced by both parties, and having patiently listened to the arguments and explanations which have been offered, as well by the prosecutor as by the accused, does solemnly judge and declare that the charge against the said Rev. P. B. has not been proved. And

The Presbytery further declares and says that it has been deeply pained by the manifestation, on the part of the prosecutor, of an unkind and unchristian spirit towards the accused, for which it finds no apology in the conduct of the accused, either as it has been displayed before the Presbytery, during the painful trial now terminated, or as it has been proved by the testimony of the witnesses who have been examined by the parties in the case: and

The Presbytery, therefore, feels constrained to admonish the said prosecutor, and to rebuke the temper in which he has conducted the prosecution; and to exhort him solemnly to review his course in this whole procedure; to be reconciled to his brother; and to cultivate that blessed charity which "thinketh no evil," and which "rejoiceth not in iniquity, but rejoiceth in the truth."

[If the conduct of the prosecutor, on the other hand, has been of that charitable and conciliatory character which makes it evident that he has not been actuated by improper and unchristian motives in the prosecution, the second part of the "Finding" should be expressed in the following terms:—]

The Presbytery further declares and says that it has been highly gratified with the kind and Christian temper of the prosecutor, which has been exhibited throughout the whole trial now so happily terminated; and that it is happy to feel, and to testify, that it is not called upon to pronounce any censure upon him.

The case is dismissed, therefore, with the hope, which the Presbytery rejoices to entertain, that the parties will henceforth cherish, each to the other, those sentiments of fraternal confidence and affection with which they are both regarded by their brethren of the Presbytery.

After which,

The members of the Judicatory united in prayer and thanksgiving to Almighty God for the grateful issue to which he has been pleased to conduct these proceedings.

[One class of cases yet remains. It is said in the "Book of Discipline," chap. iii. sec. vi., "That in consequence of a report, which does not fully amount to a *general rumor*, a slandered individual may request a judicial investigation, which it may be the duty of the Judicatory to institute."

Such a request may be presented orally, or in writing, at the option of the individual making it. It is better, however, that all such communications should be made in writing, and as definitely as possible. It may be introduced to the Judicatory in the manner following:—]

The Moderator called the attention of the Presbytery to a communication which has been placed in his hands by the Rev. J. P., a member of this Presbytery, with a request that it should be presented to the Judicatory for its consideration.

The paper was read for the information of the Presbytery, and,

After mature deliberation, it was

Ordered, That it be entered upon the minutes.

The communication is in the following words:—

B——, January 1, 18—.

To the Rev. A. B.,

Moderator of the Presbytery of H.

REV. AND DEAR SIR:—

You are requested to present to the Judicatory over which you preside, the following statement, for its consideration, and for such action as, in its wisdom, it may judge to be necessary and proper.

The undersigned has learned that a report is in circulation, to the injury of his Christian and ministerial standing, which alleges that he has appropriated to his private use funds intrusted to him for a special purpose, [or, state the purpose,] and that, when an explanation was sought from him, he had equivocated in his reply, and had manifested tokens of conscious guilt, even when denying the truth of the charge.

The undersigned has learned that the report further alleges that he has been guilty in a similar manner in several instances, and in each of his former pastoral charges; and that credit is given to the report to such an extent as seriously to affect his Christian and ministerial reputation. In proof of which, it is only necessary to state that when, recently, the congregation in —— was about to present to him a call to become its pastor, this report found its way, and was circulated, among the people of that congregation, and that its influence upon them, as he is credibly informed, was such as to lead them to relinquish their purpose of inviting him to settle among them in the ministry.

Now, inasmuch as the undersigned is unable to trace this report to any responsible individual, from whom he might demand a retraction of the charge; and inasmuch as the report has been so extensively circulated that no private measures can relieve him from the obloquy which has been cast upon him; and inasmuch, moreover, as certain friends, in whom he reposes the greatest confidence, have advised him to this course; the undersigned respectfully requests that "a judicial investigation" may be instituted by his Presbytery,—the constitutional defender of his Christian and ministerial reputation,—that he may have the opportunity to disprove before his brethren the unworthy charges with which rumor has connected his name.

All of which is respectfully submitted.

(Signed)

J. P., a member of the Presbytery of H.

The following minute was then adopted, namely:—

The Presbytery is disposed fully to recognize the right of a member to solicit a judicial investigation of rumors seriously affecting his Christian and ministerial reputation, and to admit that, according to the "Book of Discipline," chapter iii. section vi., "it *may be* the duty of the Judicatory to institute such an investigation."

At the same time, the Presbytery, as the guardian of the reputation of its members, is clearly of the opinion that such an investigation ought not to be instituted without a manifest necessity; and that, when it does appear to be necessary, the greatest caution should be exercised in every stage of the proceedings, lest evil rather than good should be the result, and lest the reputation of a brother should be only the more seriously compromitted by the very measures which were undertaken in its defence.

It is deemed prudent, therefore, in the first instance, to appoint a committee to ascertain whether the rumors, alleged by the Rev. J. P. to be circulating to the injury of his Christian and ministerial reputation, are so widely spread, and so serious in their nature, as to make it the duty of the Presbytery to institute the investigation which he has requested.

The Rev. Messrs. E. F. and G. H., and Mr. J. K., elder, were appointed the committee contemplated in the foregoing minute; and they were directed, if the circumstances should seem to demand such an investigation, to prepare the charge in proper form, and to report to the Presbytery at an adjourned meeting.

[At the adjourned meeting the report of the committee may be to the effect that it finds no sufficient reason for instituting an investigation of the rumor, and that it recommends to the Presbytery to dismiss the whole subject; or, if the members are satisfied that an investigation ought to be had, the committee may present its report in the following manner:—]

The committee which was appointed at the last meeting of the Presbytery to ascertain the nature and prevalence of the rumors in the case of the Rev. J. P., respectfully reports:—

That its first efforts were directed to ascertain whether the reports referred to by Mr. P. *do* prevail to such an extent as to justify the Presbytery in commencing a judicial process on the ground of "*common fame.*"

From the best information which the members of the committee were able to obtain, without incurring the danger of *themselves* bruiting the matter, they were satisfied that the rumors are both extensive and clamorous throughout the bounds of several of our own congregations, and in certain portions of an adjoining Presbytery, as well as among some of the neighboring congregations connected with other branches of the Church of Christ.

Your committee next proceeded to examine the facts bearing upon *the merits of the case*, in order to determine whether the rumors are "so serious in their nature" as to make it the duty of the Presbytery to institute a judicial investigation of Mr. P's. conduct in the premises.

To this inquiry the committee gave its most earnest attention. And the result to which it has been led, is a deep conviction that the Presbytery ought—without unnecessary delay—to give Mr. P. the opportunity of disproving the rumors so extensively believed, to the injury of his Christian and ministerial reputation.

The character of the ministry in general, also, and the interests of religion, in the judgment of your committee, do certainly require a judicial investigation of the case, in order that the rumors, if untrue, may be disproved and put to silence.

In accordance, therefore, with the direction of the Presbytery, the committee has prepared, and now presents, the following

CHARGE.

Common fame charges the Rev. J. P., a member of this Presbytery, with *unchristian and unministerial conduct*, as the same is set forth in the following specifications, namely:—

Specification First.

[Here insert the specifications, and append the names of the witnesses, after the models given in the preceding pages. Then conclude the report as follows:]—

All of which is respectfully submitted.

By order of the Committee,

(Signed) E. F., *Chairman.*

The report of the committee was accepted.

[Then proceed as in any other case in which "common fame is the accuser." That an investigation has been instituted *at the request* of an individual, who claims that he has been *slandered*, furnishes no reason why the "actual process," when once commenced, should not be conducted regularly in all respects. It is a "judicial investigation," whatever its origin; and the object of the Judicatory should be to ascertain *the truth* in regard to the matters charged; and *not*—as it has sometimes seemed to be supposed, by the party implicated, that it was merely to exculpate the accused, and to shield him, by the semblance of a trial, from the just reproach of his own misconduct.]

[If the accused person shall fail to appear before the Judicatory in obedience to the first citation, nothing further can be done than to ascertain from the clerk that the citation has been "duly served," and to authorize and issue the "second citation," giving notice to the prosecutor, or "Committee of Prosecution," and to all the witnesses, of the time and place of the next meeting, and issuing the second citation to any witness who may have failed to appear.

By chapter iv. section xii. of the "Book of Discipline," "at least ten days" must be given to an accused person, or a witness, "to obey the *first* citation. But, for the *second*, it is only necessary to allow 'sufficient time' for a seasonable and convenient compliance with the citation."

When the time appointed in the second citation shall have arrived, if the accused person still fails to appear, the Judicatory (Session) should proceed in the following manner:]—

It having been ascertained that the citations, ordered at the last meeting, "have been duly served on the persons for whom they were intended," and

Mr. B., the "Committee of Prosecution," being present, and ready for trial, although the accused still failed to appear,

The Session determined to proceed to the investigation of the "business assigned for trial."

The Moderator then "solemnly announced from the chair, that the body is about to pass to the consideration of the business assigned for trial, and enjoined on the members to recollect and regard their high character, as judges of a court of Jesus Christ, and the solemn duty in which they are about to act."

Whereupon, after protracted deliberation, the following minute was adopted, namely :—

Whereas, It appears, to the satisfaction of the Session, that J. B. G. has been duly cited, the second time, to appear before the Judicatory to answer to the charge laid against him on the ground of common fame; and

Whereas, He still refuses to obey the lawful summons of the Session, to which, as a member of this church, he is properly responsible, in the discipline of Christ's house:

Now, therefore, be it *Resolved,*

1. That the said J. B. G. ought to be, and he hereby is, solemnly "excluded from the communion of the church, for his contumacy, until he repent."

2. That, according to the "Book of Discipline," chapter iv. section xiii., the Session "will proceed to take the testimony in his case, as if he were present."

3. That Mr. F., a member of this Judicatory, be "assigned," according to the rule referred to in the preceding resolution, "to manage the defence" of the said J. B. G.

The charge, with its specifications, as recorded on page 69 of these minutes, was then read; and

Mr. F., representing the accused by the appointment of the Session, entered, *pro forma*, the plea of Not Guilty.

The "Committee of Prosecution" proceeded to address the Judicatory, presenting his view, &c.

[Proceed, now, as in the trial before given; and, after the testimony of all the witnesses shall have been taken and recorded, let the following minute be adopted, namely:—]

The testimony of all the witnesses in the case of J. B. G. having now been taken, and recorded, with the advantage to the accused of the cross-examination of each witness by Mr. F., the member "assigned to manage the defence," in the wilful absence of the said J. B. G.; and

The Session having, as before recorded, excluded the said J. B. G. from the communion of the church, because of his contumacy in refusing to appear and answer to the charge preferred against him on the ground of common fame;

The cause of religion and sound morals is vindicated, so far as, by the Constitution and laws of the Presbyterian Church, it lies in the power of the Session to do.

"The business assigned for trial" is, there-

fore, now left, without any decision in regard to the guilt or innocence of the accused, as concerning the matters charged against him; but with the earnest prayer that God, in the abundance of his grace, and for the sake of our Blessed Mediator and Advocate, the Lord Jesus Christ, will lead our offending brother to repentance, as for all his sins, so for this, also, his sin of contumacy, in "refusing to hear the Church."

[We have now finished all the "forms" in the *original* trial of cases of discipline that we propose to give. We have not, indeed, *carried through* a trial, in all its details; because it is manifestly impossible to furnish within any reasonable limits—if at all, in imaginary cases—the proper forms for recording all the questions, and "points of order," and decisions, which may be called forth in the progress of a judicial investigation. Still, it is believed that, in all essential respects, this part of our Manual will be found to be complete.

Before we proceed to the subject of Appellate Jurisdiction, it is thought to be the more convenient arrangement, as it is the more natural, to furnish in this place the necessary "forms" for the several *citations* which the "Book" requires in the process of Discipline.]

Citations.

I. *To the Prosecutor*

G——, January 1, 18—.

To the Rev. G. T.

SIR:—

You are hereby cited to be and appear before the Presbytery of H., at the Presbyterian Church in C., on Tuesday, the —— day of ——, at eleven o'clock, A. M., then and there to prosecute the charge against the Rev. P. B., by you presented to the Presbytery, on the —— day of ——; to the end that "the matter may be fully heard and decided."

By order of the Presbytery of H.
A. B., *Stated Clerk.*

II. *To the Person Accused.*

E——, January 1, 18—.

To J. B. G.

SIR:—

You are hereby cited to be and appear before the Session of the Presbyterian Church in this village, at the lecture-room of the said church, on Tuesday, the —— day of ——, at two o'clock, P. M., then and there to answer to the charge preferred against you by common fame; [or, by C. S.;] a copy of which charge, with the several specifications under it, and with the names of the witnesses appended to it, was given to you on Tuesday, the —— day of ——; to the end that "the matter may be fully heard and decided."

By order of the Session.
A. B., *Moderator*, [or *Clerk*.]

III. *Second Citation to the Person Accused.*

[The second citation to the person accused should not differ from the form given for the first citation, except in the necessary change of the dates, and in the *addition* to it of the following paragraph :]—

This being your "second citation," you are hereby informed, according to the direction of the "Book of Discipline," chapter iv. section x., that if you fail to appear at the time and place above named, you will "be excluded from the communion of the church, for your contumacy, until you repent;" and, according to the xiii. section of the same chapter, that the Session, "besides censuring you for your contumacy, will, after assigning some person to manage your defence, proceed to take the testimony in your case, as if you were present."

IV. *Third Citation to a Minister Accused.*

[The first and second citations to a minister need not differ, except circumstantially, from those addressed to a private person; unless it should be thought proper to refer to chapter v.

section xi., instead of, or in addition to, the reference to chapter iv. section x.

After the proceedings in the Presbytery, consequent upon the failure of the accused to obey the second citation,—after the testimony has been taken and recorded, as directed in chapter iv. section xiii.,—if the minister is "accused of atrocious crime," it is provided that he may be cited a *third* time. In this citation the same form should be adopted as directed for the first,—see No. II., above,—with the addition of the following paragraph :]—

This being your "*third* citation," you are hereby informed that, according to the "Book of Discipline," chapter v. section xi., if you shall fail to appear at the time and place above named, you will be "deposed as contumacious."

V. *To a Witness.*

E——, January 31, 18—.

To Mr. B. A.

SIR :—

You are hereby cited to be and appear before the Session of the Presbyterian Church in this village, in the lecture-room of the said church, on Tuesday, the —— day of ——, at two o'clock, P. M., then and there to give your testimony in regard to the matters charged against J. B. G. on the ground of common fame, [or, by C. S.]

By order of the Session.

A. B., *Moderator,* [or *Clerk.*]

VI. *Second Citation to a Witness.*

[The second citation to a witness should be after the model above given,—see No. V.,—with the *addition* of the following paragraph:]—

This being your "second citation," you are hereby informed, according to the direction of the "Book of Discipline," chapter iv. section x., that if you fail to appear at the time and place above named, you will "be excluded from the communion of the church, for your contumacy, until you repent."

Appellate Jurisdiction.

There are four different ways provided in the "Book of Discipline," chapter vii., in which a "decision which is formed in any Judicatory, except the highest, may be carried before a superior Judicatory" for review. These various modes are so fully described in the several sections of this chapter, that it will not be necessary to occupy much space in these pages with "forms" adapted to them.

General Review and Control.

In the *first* mode—that of "*General Review and Control*"—the initiative is taken by the superior Judicatory, and all the proceedings of the inferior, of every kind, are brought under its cognizance.

The ordinary operation of this mode will be found sufficiently exhibited in the "Form for the Records of a Presbytery," and also in that "for the Records of a Synod."

In regard to a case such as is supposed in the vi. sub-section of the section on "Review," it is proper to say that the forms already given for the citation of individuals will suggest the proper form for a citation which may be addressed to an inferior Judicatory; and that the minutes, where the matter to be recorded requires that they should be peculiar in their form, must be so much modified by the circumstances which they are intended to set forth, that it is evidently impossible to provide for them beforehand.

A Reference.

The *second* mode of carrying up a case is by *a "Reference."* In this mode, the inferior Judicatory either invokes the advice of the superior in regard to some question which has arisen in a judicial investigation, or refers the whole case to the superior Judicatory for adjudication.

In the former case, the minute on the records of the inferior Judicatory should be :—]

A question here arose, whether, &c.; [state the question definitely.]

After a protracted discussion, it was

Resolved, That this question be referred to the Presbytery, at its next meeting, for its advice in regard to the proper decision of the point involved.

[The form in which this reference is laid before the superior Judicatory may be as follows :—]

The Session of the church in E. respectfully refers the following question to the Presbytery of H., for its advice in regard to the manner in which it should be decided :—

Does the "Book of Discipline" allow? &c.; [here let the question which is referred be stated definitely.]

[In the superior Judicatory the record should be :—]

An overture was received from the Session of the church in E., containing the following question, which the Session refers to this body for its advice :—

"Does the 'Book of Discipline' allow?" &c.

The "Reference" was made the order of the day for to-morrow morning at ten o'clock; [or, was put upon the docket for future consideration; or, was committed to the Rev. Messrs. A. and B., and Mr. C., elder, to consider and report during the present sessions.]

[In the subsequent treatment of the subject by the superior Judicatory, it is not probable that any peculiar "form of minute" will be required.]

[When the inferior Judicatory refers a case for *adjudication* by the superior, it should place upon its own records a full statement of the reasons which have induced it to make the "reference;" and its overture to the superior Judicatory should be in the following form :—]

The Session of the church in E. respectfully represents to the Presbytery of H. that, in the case of, [state the case,] in consequence of, [state the reasons,] it appears to be "highly desirable" to remove the matter from the jurisdiction of the Session to that of the Presbytery. The propriety of this course will more fully appear from the minutes of the Session, a certified copy of which is herewith presented.

The Session asks leave, therefore, "totally to relinquish the decision, and to submit the whole cause to the final judgment of the Presbytery."

[If the superior Judicatory entertains the "reference," it will proceed in the investigation of the case according to the forms already given.]

AN APPEAL.

[In the *third* mode of carrying up a case to a superior Judicatory, namely, by *appeal*, a party to a judicial investigation, against whom the inferior Judicatory has given its decision, applies to the superior to review and reverse the said decision of the lower court.

The trial of an appeal is exhibited in the "Form for the Records of a Synod."

The *form* of an appeal is here given, as follows:—]

E——, January 1, 18—.

To the Rev. R. B.,

Moderator of the Synod of N.

REV. AND DEAR SIR:—

The appeal of the undersigned from the decision of the Presbytery of A. in his case, respectfully represents that, on the —— day of ——, in the year 18—, the said Presbytery of A. did pronounce against him the judgment herein set forth below, as the result of its investigation of certain charges affecting the Christian and ministerial standing of your appellant, which had been presented to the Presbytery by the Rev. G. T.; [or which had been prepared by a committee of the said Presbytery, on the ground of "common fame."]

The decision of the Presbytery is expressed in the following words, namely:—

[Here insert the decision of the Presbytery as recorded on page 88 of this volume.]

From this decision of the Presbytery aforesaid the undersigned appeals to the Synod of N., and respectfully requests the Synod to reverse the decision of the inferior Judicatory, and to restore him to the full exercise of the functions of his office, from which he claims that he has been unjustly suspended.

And for this appeal he presents the following reasons; all of which he respectfully asks that opportunity may be afforded him to vindicate and prove to the entire satisfaction of the Synod.

I. Because, &c.

[Here let all the reasons on which the appellant relies to sustain his appeal follow, in their most natural order, (see "Book of Discipline," chapter vii. section iii. sub-section iii.,) and let the whole be closed in the following manner:—]

And now, Mr. Moderator, for all these reasons, I appeal from the decision of the Presbytery aforesaid to the judgment of the reverend body over which you preside, and solicit at your hands the justice which, as it appears to me, was withheld from me in the court below.

I am, reverend and dear sir,

With very great respect,

Yours, &c.,

(Signed) P. B.

COMPLAINT.

[In the *fourth* mode of bringing a case to the notice of a superior Judicatory,—by *complaint*,—some individual, *not a party* in the case, complains of the course pursued or of the decision made by the body before which the case was investigated, and asks the superior Judicatory to review the proceedings, and to rectify the wrong which it is claimed has been done.

The *complaint* differs from an appeal chiefly in this: that the appeal must be made by *a party* to an investigation, claiming to have been injured by the decision of the inferior Judicatory. The *complaint* may be brought by *any* person who is *not* a party.

The principles involved in the "complaint" are exhibited in the iv. section of the vii. chapter of the "Book of Discipline;" but the appropriate forms of procedure would differ so little from those required in the case of an appeal, that it seems to be unnecessary to furnish them.]

Dissents and Protests.

[The "Book of Discipline," chapter viii., defines the nature of these important safeguards of the rights of a minority, and settles the principles on which they are to be employed. The following "forms" have been carefully adapted to the directions of that chapter.

A dissent by a single member of any Judicatory may be recorded in the following terms:—]

The Rev. E. C. desired that his respectful dissent from this decision [or, resolution, or, opinion] may be entered upon the minutes.

[A protest, even by a single individual, should be preceded by a notice, which, in all ordinary cases, ought to be given immediately after the decision against which the member desires to protest. Sufficient time can then be taken to prepare the protest with its reasons. The minute should be:—]

The Rev. E. C. gave notice of his intention to enter his protest against this decision [or, proceeding].

[If the minority is composed of several members, the notice may be recorded in the following manner:—]

The Rev. E. C., for himself, and for others who may wish to join with him, gave notice of their intention to enter their dissent from [or, protest against] this decision.

[When the dissent or protest shall have been prepared and signed by all who desire to join in it, it should be introduced upon the record in the following manner:—]

In accordance with the notice which was given yesterday, [or, which was heretofore given,] the following dissent [or, protest] was presented; and, having been read, it was ordered to be entered upon the minutes:—

[The dissent may be expressed in the language which follows:—]

The undersigned ask leave to record upon the minutes their respectful dissent from the decision [or, resolution, or, action] of the majority of the Presbytery [or, Synod] in regard to [here let the matter be indicated as briefly as possible].

(Signed) E. C. B. Y. R. G., &c.

[The following is a suitable form for a protest with reasons:—]

The undersigned respectfully ask leave to record upon the minutes of the Presbytery [or, Synod] their solemn protest against the decision [or, action] of the majority in reference to [here indicate the matter], for the following reasons, namely:—

I. [Here present the reasons and arguments which have influenced the minds of the members protesting, and add the signatures of all who desire to unite in making the protest.]

[If the Judicatory shall be of opinion that the protest ought to receive an answer, in order that the "principles or reasonings" which influenced the action of the majority may be accurately represented, a committee for this purpose should be appointed, the members composing it being taken from the majority, thus:—]

The Rev. Messrs. A. and B. were appointed a committee "to draw up an answer" to the foregoing protest; [or, if the committee shall not be appointed until after the transaction of other business shall have intervened, to the protest of the Rev. E. C. and others.]

[When the answer to the protest is introduced, the minute should be in the following form:—]

The committee which was appointed "to draw up an answer to the protest" of the Rev. E. C. and others, presented its report, which was adopted as the answer of the majority of the Presbytery, [or, Synod,] and is as follows:—

The action of the Presbytery, against which the Rev. E. C. and others have entered their protest, is not justly liable to the objections urged by the members protesting, for the following reasons, namely: [or, as will appear from the following considerations, namely:]

I. [The reasons or considerations should be so framed as to answer all the arguments of the protest; yet they should be presented as briefly as possible.]

[If the members who signed the protest should "consider the answer of the majority as imputing to them opinions or conduct which they disavow," or as doing injustice to the arguments which they had advanced in their protest, they may desire to modify in some respects the protest which they have entered; and the minute should be:—]

The members, to whose protest the foregoing answer was made by the majority of the Presbytery, requested "leave to take back their protest," that they might "modify it in such manner as to render it more agreeable to their views." And

Their request was granted.

[The modified protest having been presented, the record should state that]

The modified protest of the Rev. E. C. and others was presented; and, having been read, it was ordered to be entered upon the minutes in the words following:—

The undersigned, &c.

[If the "alteration" which is made in the protest shall seem to require "a corresponding alteration in the answer of the majority," the alteration may be made in the house, or the paper may be referred back to the committee for the purpose, as follows:—]

The modifications in the protest as now presented having rendered proper "a corresponding alteration in the answer of the majority,"

The original answer was referred again to the committee which drew it up, for the purpose of making the necessary modifications.

[When the committee shall report the modified answer to the protest, the record may be:—]

The committee on the "answer to the protest of the Rev. E. C. and others" presented the document, as now modified in accordance with the alterations which have been made in the protest, and it was adopted, as follows:—

The action of the Presbytery, &c.

[When a protest is "accompanied with a complaint to a superior Judicatory"—as provided in the chapter "of Dissents and Protests," sec. iv.—the "form" may be as follows:—]

The undersigned ask leave to record their solemn protest against the decision of a majority of the Presbytery in regard to [here state the matter], and give notice of their intention to complain of the same to the Synod of N., at its next meeting, for the following reasons, namely:

I., &c., [Here present the reasons, as before directed.]

[If the complainants desire more time than they can command during the sessions of the Judicatory, to arrange the reasons for their complaint, they are permitted, by the section "Of Complaints," sub-section iv., to present them to the Moderator "within ten days" after "the rising of the Judicatory." If they design to avail themselves of this privilege, the last clause of the above notice—"for the following reasons, namely:"—should be replaced by the following words:—The reasons for the complaint they will "lodge with the Moderator" within ten days after the rising of the Presbytery.]

Form for the Records of a Synod.

SYNOD OF N——.

A.D. 18—.

The Synod of N—— met in the Presbyterian Church in H., on Tuesday, October 17th, A.D. 18—, at seven o'clock P.M., and was opened with a sermon by the Moderator, the Rev. H. L., of the Presbytery of R., from 2 Timothy i. 13:—"Hold fast the form of sound words, which thou hast heard of me, in faith and love which is in Christ Jesus."

After the sermon, the Moderator offered prayer, and presided during the constituting of the Synod.

The roll was made out, and is as follows:—

MINISTERS.	CHURCHES.	ELDERS.
	Of the Presbytery of H.	
J. D.		
R. A.	C.	P. N.
A. B.	B.	L. F.
	R.	*G. S.
	Of the Presbytery of B	
J. F.	L.	D. E.
R. B.	F.	*W. T.
*B. S.		
	N.	G. R.

* Not present at the opening of the Synod.

[The entire roll of the members in attendance upon the

Of the Presbytery of R.

H. L.	P.	J. B.
S. M.	L.	*C. G.
*I. G.		

Of the Presbytery of S.

R. K.,	W.	F. P.
M. O.	T.	*B. N.

Ministers.—47. *Elders.*—32.

The Rev. R. B., of the Presbytery of B., was elected Moderator; and the Rev. Messrs. O. J. and D. P. were elected temporary Clerks.

The Committee of Arrangements presented the following report, which was adopted, namely:—

The committee recommends the following arrangement for the devotional and business sessions of the Synod:—

1. That the Synodical Sermon be preached in the church, on Wednesday evening, at half-past seven o'clock.

2. That the Sacrament of the Lord's Supper be celebrated in the church, on Thursday, at half-past two o'clock P.M.

---

sessions of the Synod should be inserted. The members coming after the opening session will be recognised in their proper places in the minutes; but they should be indicated in the roll by an asterisk prefixed to their names, as in the text, and referring to a note at the bottom of the page, as above.]

* Not present at the opening Session of the Synod.

3. That the Synodical Prayer-Meeting be holden in the church, on Thursday evening, at half-past seven o'clock; and

4. That the business sessions of the Synod be holden in the lecture-room of this church, as follows:—

The morning session to commence at half-past eight o'clock, and to continue until half-past twelve;

The afternoon session to commence at half-past two o'clock, and to continue until half-past five; and

The evening session to commence at half-past seven o'clock.

The Synod then adjourned, to meet to-morrow morning, at half-past eight o'clock, in the lecture-room of this church.

Concluded with prayer by the Moderator.

WEDNESDAY, October 18, 18—

The Synod met, pursuant to adjournment, and engaged in devotional exercises, according to the standing rule.*

The roll was then called, and the following

---

* The Synod whose records have been taken as a guide in preparing the "Form" in the text has a standing rule requiring that its "daily sessions shall be opened with devotional exercises, to be continued at least three-fourths of an hour."

additional members were reported as being present, namely:—*

Of the Presbytery of H., Mr. G. S., elder.

Of the Presbytery of R., the Rev. J. G.; and

Of the Presbytery of S., Mr. B. N., elder.

The minutes of the opening session were read and approved; and printed copies of the minutes of the last annual meeting were distributed among the members.†

Information was received from the Rev. Messrs. S. F., G. L., P. S., D. B., J. W., H. T., and D. M., communicating the reasons of their absence from the present sessions of the Synod.

The Rev. Messrs. G. D., of the Synod of P., L. H., D.D., of the Synod of J., E. C., of the

---

* This minute is formed in accordance with another rule of the same Synod, by which members coming at any time after the opening session are required to report themselves, and their excuses, to the chairman of the Committee on Leave of Absence. The clerks enter their names upon the roll as they are reported to them by the chairman of the committee. Time otherwise consumed in hearing excuses for late attendance—in a numerous Synod, often serious in its aggregate—is thus saved; and an unpleasant interruption to business, frequently recurring, is obviated. The operation of the rule has proved to be highly satisfactory.

† If a Synod has not the useful practice of printing its minutes for circulation among its members and the churches under its care, the second clause of this minute should be replaced by the following:—"and the minutes of the last annual meeting were also read."

Berkshire Association, Mass., and A. B. L., D.D., of the Synod of A., being present, were invited to sit as corresponding members.

The docket of business was then presented and read by the Stated Clerk.

The Moderator announced the Standing Committees, as follows:—

1. *Of Bills and Overtures.*—The Rev. Drs. A., E., and M., and Messrs. A., J., and W., elders.

2. *Judicial Committee.*—The Rev. Dr. S., the Rev. Messrs. P. and H., and Messrs. B. and P., elders.

3. *On Leave of Absence.*—The Rev. Messrs. G. and C., and Dr. J., elder.

4. *On the Narrative.*—The Rev. Messrs. C., M., and W., and Messrs. G. and J., elders.

5. *On the Minutes of the General Assembly.*—The Rev. Messrs. F. and S. T., and Mr. T., elder.

On the Records of the Presbyteries.

Of H.—The Rev. Messrs. L. and C., and Mr. B., elder.

Of B.—The Rev. Messrs. T. and S., and the Hon. M. P., elder.

Of R.—The Rev. Messrs. F. and B., and Dr. R., elder.

Of S.—The Rev. Messrs. P. and A., and Mr. S., elder.

The Committee of Arrangements presented a report, recommending the following order of exercises for the celebration of the Lord's Supper on Thursday afternoon, namely:—

1. Introductory Remarks, and Hymn, by the Moderator.
2. Prayer, by the Rev. Mr. T.
3. Address, by the Rev. Dr. A.
4. Administration of the Sacrament, by the Rev. Dr. C.
5. Address, by the Rev. Mr. D.
6. Prayer, by the Rev. Dr. W.
7. Hymn, and Benediction, by the Moderator.

The committee also recommended the following order of exercises for this evening:—[Insert order.]

The recommendations of the committee were adopted.

The Treasurer of the Synod presented his annual report; and, having been read, it was referred to Mr. J. and Dr. W., elders, for examination.

Mr. P., elder, was appointed a committee to receive from the several Presbyteries the amount assessed upon them in the standing rule to meet the contingent expenses of the Synod.*

* An assessment upon the several Presbyteries, arranged according to the number and ability of the churches under the care of each, has been found to be the most satisfactory method of obtaining the funds required for the incidental expenses of the Synod.

The next annual meeting of the Synod was appointed to be holden in the First Presbyterian Church in N., on the third Tuesday in October, A.D. 18—, at seven o'clock P.M.; and the Rev. Drs. A. and B., the Rev. Mr. C., and Messrs. D. and E., and Dr. F., elders, were appointed the Committee of Arrangements.

The Rev. Dr. A., the Rev. Mr. C., and Mr. H., elder, were appointed a committee to nominate a preacher, and to propose a subject for the sermon to be delivered during the next annual meeting of the Synod.

It was made the order of the day for to-morrow morning at ten o'clock to hear the statistical reports of the several Presbyteries, and the Narratives of the State of Religion within their bounds.

The committee on ——, appointed at the last annual meeting of the Synod, reported progress, and requested to be continued; and also that Messrs. G. and H., elders, may, for reasons which were briefly assigned, be added to the committee as at present constituted.

The report was accepted, and the requests of the committee were granted.

The committee appointed at the last annual meeting to consider the subject of —— presented a report, which was accepted.

On the question of adopting the report, a protracted discussion arose;—pending which,

A recess was taken until half-past two o'clock.

After the recess, the following additional members were reported as being present, namely:—

Of the Presbytery of H., the Rev. B. J. and Mr. R. T., elder;

Of the Presbytery of R., Mr. C. G., elder.

The unfinished business of the morning, namely, the report of the committee on the subject of ——, was then taken up for consideration; and,

After further discussion,

In view of the importance of the subject, the report was referred to the Rev. Dr. S., the Rev. Mr. H., and Messrs. B. and J., elders, to give it further consideration, and to report at the next annual meeting of the Synod.

The committee to audit the Treasurer's accounts reported that it finds them to be correct, as compared with the vouchers accompanying them.

The report was accepted.

The Committee of Bills and Overtures reported that an overture—No. I.—had been presented to it, proposing that measures should be taken with a view to the division of this

Body into two Synods. The committee recommends that no action should be taken on this subject:—and

The recommendation of the committee was unanimously adopted.

The committee also reported that it had received an overture—No. II.—in reference to the erection of a new Presbytery, to be composed of portions of the Presbyteries of B. and R.

In regard to the subject of this overture, the committee is of the opinion that there exists no occasion for the exercise of the Synod's power "to erect new Presbyteries," in the absence of any request to that effect from the Presbyteries concerned. The committee therefore recommends that no action should be taken in the premises by the Synod.

The recommendation was adopted.

The committee further reported,

Overture III. In our "Form of Government," chap. xiii. sec. ii., do the words "church" and "congregation" mean the same body?

The committee recommends that this inquiry be answered in the affirmative.

This report was accepted, and referred to the Rev. Messrs. M. and N., to prepare a minute which shall express the judgment of the Synod upon the subject.

A recess was then taken until half-past seven o'clock, in the church.

At half-past seven o'clock, the Rev. R. N. B. preached, by appointment, on "The Doctrine of Regeneration," from John i. 13:—"Which were born, not of blood, nor of the will of the flesh, nor of the will of man, but of God;" and the exercises were conducted according to the previous arrangement of the Synod.

After the services,

The Synod adjourned, to meet to-morrow morning, at half-past eight o'clock, in the lecture-room.

Concluded with prayer.

THURSDAY, October 19, 18—

The Synod met, pursuant to adjournment, and engaged in devotional exercises, according to the standing rule.

The calling of the roll was dispensed with.

Mr. C. G., elder, *of the Presbytery of R.*, was reported as being present.

The minutes of the proceedings of yesterday were read and approved.

The Committee of Arrangements made a report, recommending the following order of exercises for the Synodical Prayer-Meeting at half-past seven o'clock this evening:—[Insert Report.]

The report was adopted.

The committee which was appointed to examine the Minutes of the General Assembly reported that it would call the attention of the Synod to the following items, namely:—

1. On page 482: The recommendation by the Assembly of the observance of the first Monday in January as a day of prayer for the conversion of the world, and also of the last Thursday in February as a day of prayer for colleges.

2. On page 496: The subject of the "Church-Erection Fund" of the General Assembly.

3. On page 503: The resolution of the Assembly on the subject of Temperance.

4. On page 511: The action in regard to the Presbyterian Publication Commitee

5. On page 513: The subject of the Education of Young Men for the Office of the Gospel Ministry. And,

6. On page 538: The recommendation of the General Assembly of 1821, That "all the churches under our care observe the *afternoon or evening previous to the meeting* of the General Assembly as A SEASON OF SPECIAL PRAYER to Almighty God for his blessing" upon its sessions.

The report of the committee was accepted.

The first item of the report was then taken up for consideration; and the Synod recommended to all the churches under its care to observe the first Monday in January, and the last Thursday in February, in the manner contemplated in the recommendation of the General Assembly.

The second, fourth, and fifth items of the report were put upon the docket for future consideration.

The third item of the report—on the subject of *Temperance*—was taken up, and the resolution of the Assembly was adopted, in the words following, namely:—

[The insertion of the minute itself is not deemed to be essential to the purpose of these "forms."]

The sixth item of the report—respecting *special prayer for the General Assembly*—was then taken up for consideration, and the following resolution was adopted:—

Resolved, That the Synod heartily concurs in this important recommendation of the Assembly of 1821, and would express its earnest desire that the observance of the appointed season of special prayer in behalf of each General Assembly may be revived.

The Committee of Bills and Overtures reported,

Overture IV. May an accused person who fails to appear for trial, and is proved to be guilty of the charges alleged against him, be sentenced on evidence taken in his absence?

This overture was put upon the docket for future consideration.

The Synod then proceeded to the order of the day. The statistical reports of the several Presbyteries, and the Narratives of the State of Religion within their bounds, were read; and the latter were referred to the Committee on the Narrative of the Synod.

The Judicial Committee reported the appeal of M. N. from the decision of the Presbytery of A. as having been regularly conducted on the part of the appellant, and recommended that it be taken up in the order prescribed in the "Book of Discipline," chap. vii. sec. iii. subsections viii. and ix.

The report was adopted; and

It was made the order of the day, for this afternoon, after the services of the communion, to take up the said appeal.

The second item of the report of the Committee on the Minutes of the General Assembly, respecting the Assembly's "*Church-Erection Fund*," was taken up for consideration.

A circular letter from the trustees of the fund was read, and, after discussion,

The Rev. Messrs. B. and O., and Mr. P., elder, were appointed a committee to prepare a minute which shall embody the views of the Synod as expressed in this discussion, and to report the same during the present sessions.

The Committee on the Records of the Presbyteries of H., B., R., and F. severally reported, recommending that the books be approved as far as written.

These reports were adopted.

The Committee on the Records of the Presbytery of S. reported that the Book of Records has not been in the house during the present sessions of the Synod;—Whereupon

The committee was discharged.

The Committee on the Records of the Presbytery of A. requested leave to withhold its report until after the action of the Synod in the judicial case which has been reported shall have been completed.

The request was granted.

The committee which was appointed to nominate a preacher, and to propose a subject for the sermon to be delivered during the next annual meeting of the Synod, reported, recommending that the Rev. O. P. be appointed the preacher, and that the Rev. R. S., D.D., be his alternate. The committee proposed also the following subject for the discourse, namely:—"The Doctrine of the Divine Decrees; particularly that of Election."

The recommendations in this report were adopted.

The fourth item in the report of the Committee on the Minutes of the General Assembly—referring to the *Presbyterian Publication Committee*—which had been put upon the docket, was then taken up for consideration; and

The following resolutions were adopted:—

Resolved, [Engross the resolutions.]

The fifth item of the report, on the subject of *Education for the Ministry*, was taken from the docket; and,

After a brief discussion,

The following minute was adopted, namely:—

Whereas, in the judgment of this Synod, the subject, &c.

[Here proceed to engross the preamble and resolutions on this subject.]

A recess was then taken until half-past two o'clock, in the church.

At half-past two o'clock, the Sacrament of the Lord's Supper was administered in the church, and the services were conducted according to the previous arrangement.

After the services,

The Synod retired to the lecture-room and resumed the transaction of business.

The committee appointed to receive the assessments for the incidental expenses of the

Synod reported that he had received from all the Presbyteries the amount of the assessment, as directed by the standing rule, the total sum received being $——.

The report was accepted; and it was

Ordered, That the amount be placed in the hands of the Treasurer.

The resolution adopting the report of the Committee on the Records of the Presbytery of R. was reconsidered; and

The following minute was adopted as a substitute, namely:—

The minutes of the Presbytery of R. were approved as far as written, with the following exception:—

On page 205 a record is made of a resolution to proceed to the ordination of a licentiate by a *committee*, instead of by the *Presbytery* itself as required by the "Form of Government," chap. xv. sec. xii.

The Synod then proceeded to the order of the day. And

The appeal of M. N. from the decision of the Presbytery of A. was taken up.

The appellant requested that the Rev. G. K. may be assigned to him as counsel, to aid him in conducting his appeal before the Synod.

The request of the appellant was granted, and the Rev. G. K. was assigned to him as counsel.

The Moderator solemnly announced "from the chair that the Synod was about to pass to the consideration of the business assigned for trial, and enjoined upon the members to recollect and regard their high character as judges of a court of Jesus Christ, and the solemn duty in which they were about to act."

The sentence appealed from was then read.

The reasons assigned by the appellant for his appeal, and which are on record, were also read.

The whole record of the inferior Judicatories in the case, including all the testimony, was read.

The original parties were then heard, in part; and

The further consideration of the case was postponed until after the Synodical Prayer-Meeting this evening.

The Committee on the Narrative of the State of Religion within the bounds of the Synod presented its report, which was adopted and ordered to be read at the prayer-meeting this evening, and to be published. (See Appendix.)*

* If the minutes of the Synod are printed, the Narrative need not be engrossed in the records, but should be placed in an appendix, with a reference in the printed copies as in the text. If the Synod does not print its minutes, the minute in

A recess was then taken until half-past seven o'clock, in the church.

At half-past seven o'clock the Synodical Prayer-Meeting was attended in the church by the Synod, in connection with the congregation present, and the services were conducted according to the previous arrangement.

After the services,

The Synod retired to the lecture-room and resumed the transaction of business.

The committee which was appointed to prepare a minute expressing the views of the Synod in relation to the *Church-Erection Fund* of the General Assembly reported the following resolutions, which were adopted, namely:—

Resolved, That, &c.

[The resolutions should here be engrossed, being part of the records.]

The unfinished business of the afternoon, namely, the appeal of M. N., was then taken up.

The original parties were heard in continuation of their respective arguments, until they had concluded;—After which,

The Synod adjourned, to meet to-morrow morning at half-past eight o'clock.

Concluded with prayer.

---

the text should end with the words "this evening;" and the Narrative should then be inserted as in the "Form for the Records of a Presbytery" on page 24 of this Manual.

FRIDAY, October 20, 18—.

The Synod met, pursuant to adjournment, and engaged in devotional exercises, according to the standing rule.

The calling of the roll was dispensed with.

The minutes of the proceedings of yesterday were read and approved.

The Synod then resumed the consideration of the unfinished business, namely, the appeal of M. N. from the decision of the Presbytery of A.

The Session by which the case was originally tried was heard; and

The committee of the Presbytery appointed to defend its proceedings in the case was heard, until the arrival of the hour for recess, when

A recess was taken until half-past two o'clock.

After the recess, the Treasurer was directed to pay the salary of the Stated Clerk, and the janitor's bill, amounting to $——.

The unfinished business was taken up, and

The committee to defend the Presbytery was further heard.

Other members of the inferior Judicatory were also heard in explanation of the grounds of their decision, or of their dissent from it.

After all the parties had been fully heard, and the original parties and all the members of the inferior Judicatory had withdrawn from the house,

The roll was called, that every member might have an opportunity to express his opinion on the case;—After which,

The final vote was taken, and

The appeal was unanimously sustained.*

The Rev. Messrs. A. B. and C. D. were appointed a committee to prepare a minute for adoption by the Judicatory, setting forth its decision and the grounds thereof; and

The committee had leave to retire for the purpose of preparing its report.

The Rev. Drs. J. M., J. W., and H. R., and Messrs. T. K. and C. S., elders, were elected the Synod's "Committee on Church-Exten-

---

* The final vote may be merely "sustained," or "not sustained," and the record should be made accordingly, as in the text. But if the vote should be very much divided, or the principles involved in the decision seem to require it, the "yeas and nays" may be demanded by "one-third of the members present;" in which case the record should be as follows:—

The final vote was taken; and,

The yeas and nays having been ordered,

The appeal was sustained [or, the Synod refused to sustain the appeal] by the following vote, namely:—

To SUSTAIN.—*Ministers:* A. B., C. D., E. F., &c.

Elders: R. S., T. W., &c. Total vote to sustain, 54.

NOT TO SUSTAIN.—*Ministers:* G. H., J. K., &c.

Elders: O. P., S. T., &c. Total vote not to sustain, 12.

NON LIQUET.—*Ministers:* J. E., &c.

Elders: L. M., &c. Total non liquet, 5.

EXCUSED FROM VOTING.—*Ministers:* B. C., &c.

Elders: D. O., &c. Total excused from voting, 7.

sion," required by the xi. article of the General Assembly's Church-Erection Plan.

The following resolution was unanimously adopted:—

Resolved, That the thanks of the Synod be presented to the trustees of the Presbyterian church in H., for the use of their house of worship during the present sessions; to the singers, for their acceptable services; to the Committee of Arrangements, for the efficient manner in which its duties have been discharged; and to the families whose Christian hospitalities the members of the Synod have enjoyed.

The committee appointed to prepare a minute expressing the judgment of the Synod respecting the subject presented in Overture No. III. requested leave to withhold its report until the next annual meeting of the Synod.

The request was granted.

Overture IV., which had been put upon the docket, was then taken up for consideration; and, after a brief discussion,

It was referred to the Rev. Messrs. L. M. and N., and Messrs. O. and P., elders, to consider the subject, and to report at the next annual meeting of the Synod.

The Committee on Leave of Absence reported that leave of absence has been given to the following members of the Synod, namely: The Rev. Messrs. W., D., R., J., &c., and Messrs. F., G., H., &c., elders.

The committee appointed to prepare a minute setting forth the result to which the Synod has arrived in the case of the appeal of M. N. presented the following report, which was adopted, namely:—

The Synod of N., having heard and considered the appeal of M. N. from the decision of the Presbytery of A. in his case, does unanimously judge and determine that the same be, and it hereby is, sustained, on the following grounds:—

I. [Here should follow, in detail, the several reasons assigned.]

The Committee on the Records of the Presbytery of A. reported, recommending that they be approved as far as written, with the exception of so much as relates to the case of discipline which has been brought before the Synod on the appeal of M. N., and in which the appeal has been sustained and the decision of the Presbytery reversed.

The report was adopted.

The following resolution was unanimously adopted:—

Resolved, That the members of the Synod

hereby express their intention to remember each other at the throne of grace on the morning of every Lord's day.

After this resolution had been solemnly adopted, the members as a body giving their assent by rising from their seats, it was proposed to seek the blessing of God upon the engagement into which the Synod has now entered; and

A brief and appropriate prayer was accordingly offered.

The minutes of the proceedings of to-day were read and approved.

The roll was then called, and it appeared that the following members had left the Synod without leave: namely, Messrs. T., F., W., &c.

After which,

The Synod adjourned, to meet in the First Presbyterian Church in N. on the third Tuesday in October, A.D. 18—, at seven o'clock P.M.

Concluded with prayer, singing, and the benediction.

N. E. S., *Stated Clerk.*

Standing Rules.

[The following standing rules, having been approved by the experience for several years of one of our largest Synods, are given as a guide in forming a code of by-laws for the regulation of a Synod or of a Presbytery. Variations and additions will, of course, be suggested by the particular wants or experience of each Judicatory which may be disposed to adopt them.]

I. The Synod shall meet annually on the third Tuesday of October, at three o'clock P.M., at such place as shall be designated at the meeting of the previous year.

II. A Committee of Arrangements shall be appointed previously to the adjournment, yearly, who shall provide suitable accommodations for the Synod, and propose the arrangements for the devotional exercises.

III. The annual meeting of the Synod shall be opened with a sermon by the Moderator; or, in case of his failure, by some member of the Synod designated by the Committee of Arrangements.

IV. All the devotional meetings of the Synod shall be held at the place of opening the annual meeting.

V. The daily sessions of the Synod shall be opened with devotional exercises, to be continued at least three-fourths of an hour.

VI. At every annual meeting of the Synod a sermon on some topic designated by the Synod shall be preached by a minister appointed at the meeting of the previous year. The Lord's Supper also shall be celebrated. Both of these services shall be at such times as shall be proposed by the Committee of Arrangements.

VII. The permanent officers of the Synod shall be a Stated Clerk and a Treasurer, who shall continue in office during the pleasure of the Synod, and the former of whom shall receive for his services the annual sum of —— dollars.

VIII. To meet the contingent expenses of the Synod, the several Presbyteries are requested to furnish annually the amount assessed upon them in the following schedule:—

A——, $—— D——, $—— G——, $——
B——, —— E——, —— H——, ——

IX. The Stated Clerks of the several Presbyteries are charged to forward the roll of their respective bodies to the Stated

Clerk of the Synod at least one week previously to every annual meeting.

X. In addition to the statistical report required by the "Form of Government," chapter x. section ix., every Presbytery shall make an annual report, in writing, of the state of religion in their respective bodies.

XI. The minutes of the annual meeting of the Synod shall be published under the direction of the Stated Clerk, as soon as practicable after the adjournment, and a copy sent to every member of the Synod.

XII. Members of the Synod arriving at any time after the opening session shall report themselves to the chairman of the Committee on Leave of Absence, and offer their reasons for tardiness to the said committee; and their names shall be entered upon the roll by the Clerks, on the report of the chairman of the committee.

A Docket of Business.

[The docket, as prepared by the Stated Clerk before the meeting of the Judicatory, should contain all the items of routine business, all matters laid over from a former meeting, and a reference to all committees from which reports are to be received. It is not deemed necessary to present in this Manual a separate docket for a Presbytery, as the variations required to adapt the form given to any particular Judicatory will readily suggest themselves.]

DOCKET, ——, 18—.

1. Election of Moderator.
2. Election of two Temporary Clerks.
3. Printed minutes of the last annual meeting to be distributed.

[If the minutes are not printed, the third item should be, Minutes, &c. to be read.]

4. Standing committees to be appointed by the Moderator:—
   (1.) Of Bills and Overtures, to consist of three ministers and two elders; [or, four ministers and three elders;]
   (2.) Judicial Committee, to consist of three ministers and two elders;
   (3.) On Leave of Absence, to consist of two ministers and one elder;
   (4.) On the Narrative, to consist of three ministers and two elders;

(5.) On the Minutes of the General Assembly, to consist of two ministers and one elder;

(6.) On the Records of the Presbyteries, two ministers and one elder to each Presbytery.

5. Reports of the Committee of Arrangements:—

(1.) In regard to the times for the Devotional and Business Sessions;

(2.) Order of exercises for the Synodical Sermon;

(3.) Order of exercises for the Communion Service;

(4.) Order of exercises for the Synodical Prayer-Meeting.

6. Treasurer's Report to be received and read.
7. Auditing Committee to be appointed.
8. " " " report.
9. Committee to receive the assessments upon the Presbyteries to be appointed. (See VIII. Standing Rules.)
10. Committee to receive the assessments to report.
11. Place for the next annual meeting of the Synod to be appointed.
12. Committee of Arrangements for next year to be appointed.
13. Appoint committee to nominate the

preacher and the subject for the Synodical Sermon next year.

14. Committee on Preacher and Subject to report.
15. Appoint order of the day for hearing the statistical reports and the Narratives of the Presbyteries.
16. Report of the Committee on ——; Rev. Dr. G., chairman.
17. Report of the Committee on ——; Rev. J. H., chairman.
18. Report of the Committee on "Church-Extension," required by the xi. article of the General Assembly's "Church-Erection Plan;" Rev. Dr. M., chairman.
19. Appoint a similar committee for the ensuing year. It must consist of "at least five members."
20. Take order in regard to the Stated Clerk's salary, and the janitor's bill for stationery and attendance.

[To the original docket the Moderator will make additions from time to time, during the progress of the sessions, as follows:—]

21. Order of the day for Thursday, ten o'clock A.M.: statistical reports and Narratives of the Presbyteries to be read.
22. Wednesday A.M. Report of Committee on ——, unfinished at recess.

23. Overture III.: Rev. Messrs. M. and N. committee to report a minute.
24. Second item in Report on Assembly's Minutes:—"Church-Erection Fund."
25. Fourth item in Report on Assembly's Minutes:—"Presbyterian Publication Committee."
26. Fifth item in Report on Assembly's Minutes:—"Education for the Ministry."
27. Overture IV.: "Accused person failing to appear: can he be sentenced?"
28. Order of the day, after the communion services: appeal of M. N.
29. "Church-Erection Fund:"—Rev. Messrs. B. and O., and Mr. P., elder, committee to report a minute.
30. Committee on Records of the Presbytery of A. to report after the appeal shall have been issued.
31. Appeal of M. N.: further hearing after Synodical Prayer-Meeting.
32. Appeal of M. N.: further hearing, Friday morning.
33. Appeal of M. N.: further hearing, Friday P.M.
34. Committee to report a minute of the Synod's finding in the case of the appeal of M. N., Rev. Messrs. A. B. and C. D.

THE END.

INDEX.

A.

B.

C.

G.

I.

J.

L.

M.

N.

O.

P.

R.

S.

T.

V.

www.ingramcontent.com/pod-product-compliance
Lightning Source LLC
LaVergne TN
LVHW021410110826
845150LV00007B/1860

* 9 7 8 1 4 2 5 5 1 1 5 7 9 *